THE SUN WITHIN

REDISCOVER YOU

JOANNE ONG

Published by
Hasmark Publishing, judy@hasmarkservices.com

Copyright © 2017 Joanne Ong
First Edition, 2017

No part of this book may be reproduced or transmitted in any form or by any means, electronic or mechanical, including photocopying, recording or by any information storage and retrieval system, without written permission from the author, except for the inclusion of brief quotations in a review.

Disclaimer

This book is designed to provide information and motivation to our readers. It is sold with the understanding that the publisher is not engaged to render any type of psychological, legal, or any other kind of professional advice. The content of each article is the sole expression and opinion of its author, and not necessarily that of the publisher. No warranties or guarantees are expressed or implied by the publisher's choice to include any of the content in this volume. Neither the publisher nor the individual author(s) shall be liable for any physical, psychological, emotional, financial, or commercial damages, including, but not limited to, special, incidental, consequential or other damages. Our views and rights are the same: You are responsible for your own choices, actions, and results.

Permission should be addressed in writing to Joanne Ong:
www.joanne-ong.com and **www.rediscover-you.net**

Cover Design
Les Solot, Germancreative, Fiverr

Editor
Sigrid Macdonald
sigridmacdonald@rogerscom

Book Layout
Anne Karklins
annekarklins@gmail.com

ISBN-13: 978-1-988071-56-5
ISBN-10: 1988071569

"This is an eye-opening must read book! Understanding the power that comes from vulnerability, Joanne, invites you to a trip in her life sharing with you her own lessons. Accept her invitation and learn from her experiences to create a better life for yourself."

    – Anca Maria Dumitrescu, Author, "Journey – An Outlined Path to Fulfillment"

"Step into Joanne's life! Joanne shared with us her ups and downs, insights and discoveries, honest reflections and wisdoms in such a candid way you can't help but be inspired and to reflect on your own life. A must-read to all of us who are also on a journey. To follow " the contract " or to listen to the "voice"?"

    – Rafika Tan

"Joanne Ong's book "The Sun Within" is a true testament of womanhood as well as motherhood. She encapsulates the essence of spirituality through the eyes of a girl growing into a woman, and how the power of vibration can transform us into who we become as adults. Joanne tells us a story of a very real truth which will resonate with everybody who has ever felt the need to understand the 'why' of our connections, as well as the meaning of the movement of the universe through the theory of vibration--giving us stellar insight into the world around us as one moving force and energy. "The Sun Within" will take you on a journey that will cause the reader to understand the true meaning of solid connections with the people around you and our purpose in the people we attract in our lives. This book is an amazing story of perseverance, trust, and believing in our birth right, which is to be centred as well as connected to each other through love. Amazing read."

    – Pashmina P., International Best Selling Author, The Cappuccino Chronicles

"Joanne talks about her own life experiences and how life's challenges should be viewed. A powerful book and a must read."

    – Parusu Ramakrishnan

"Having known Joanne for what feels like all my life, I have always known her to be a calm and positive person. The reading of her struggles and self-awakening in "The Sun Within" is a revelation. "The Sun Within" defines and resolves the uncertainties everybody feels in their lives. It is a must read for all who are unable to define the 'incompleteness' within. If only for the stories and wit."

    – Sok Hong Teow

*This book is dedicated to my children
for helping me to realise and to pursue my spiritual path.
I sincerely hope that this will make sense to you when
you are older, and help to propel you forward in your lives,
to realise your own paths that you must undertake.
Thank you also to my husband for his
continual support in everything that I do.*

THE SUN

The bright sun
Radiates its light
To all those on earth;
Giving them life,
Giving them love,
Giving them hope.

It knows not the lives it touches;
But those whose lives have been graced
By its presence,
Are eternally grateful;
Whether they realise it or not
For its existence in their hearts,
Providing them with the growth
That they seek.

It sometimes hide behind the clouds,
But its presence is always felt;
And in the darkness of the night,
The sun continues to shine so brightly
That the moon reflects its rays of light.

As surely as the sun
Rises over the East
And sets over the West,
It is always there,
It never leaves,
It never goes away,
It only awaits
For the moment
To be rediscovered
To realise that its role
Is to be a part of life
Here on Earth.

TABLE OF CONTENTS

The Sun	6
Introduction	10
Foreword	12
PART 1 – Who Am I? My Journey So Far	**15**
Who am I?	16
Why am I here?	17
Religion and Spirituality	19
Energy	23
Soul Contracts	25
We find "ourselves" in interaction with others. – Solomon	
The Reconnection and Energetic Attractions	30
Listen to Your Instinct	32
Hear your own music. – Solomon	
Personality – Childhood	34
There comes a transition in children's lives where they have to abandon that (greater self) knowledge and root themselves in this plane. Much is lost so that much can be learned, and then re-accessed later in life. But in order for them to really understand the lessons in this place, they have to let go of the encyclopedia they brought with them. It's a closed-book test. I think you might want to look at that transition. – Solomon	
Personality – Adolescence	37
Self-worth is the understanding that you are the universe – Solomon	

Synchronicities and Detours — 40

When your desires are strong enough, you will appear to possess superhuman powers to achieve it – Napoleon Hill

Your energy is of a greater life force that is coming through you. Your thoughts are your energy manifest. It will lead you to your instinct. Your instinct is the sum total of your lives' experience. It is the encyclopedia of humanity – Solomon

Spiritual to Manifestation — 43

You are a spiritual being, you have an intellect, and you live in a physical body. – Bob Proctor

PART 2 – What Makes Me, "Me"? 47

Soul-Purpose — 48

Your mission, in a way, is to connect a spiritual heart to a spiritual existence. It's not always an easy thing you undertake. But it is the quest of life. You must allow yourself a different space. It is time to feel much more. Allow this life force to pervade you. Understand your mission. Feel it in your life. It is not of notoriety; it is of immense greatness in the satisfying nature of the way it is permitted to flow. -Solomon

Separation and Reconnection — 55

I am that, I am. – Exodus 3:14

Your purpose explains what you are doing with your life. Your vision explains how you are living your purpose. Your goals enable you to realize your vision. – Bob Proctor

Self-Discovery: The Power Within You — 59

Reconnect to the greater force that is. – Solomon

Self-Worth — 72

Self-worth is the understanding that you are the universe. – Solomon

We Are Infinite — 76

In the tapestry of life, we're all connected. – Anita Moorjani

Universal Language	79
We Are. – Dr. Wayne Dyer (through Karen Noe)	
PART 3 – The Mechanics: How it Works	83
It Is All Vibrational	84
Life caused you to create a vibrational reality. – Abraham-Hicks	
Mind-Body Relationship	89
Your Body is Your Subconscious Mind – Dr Candace Pert	
From Thought to Form	96
No thought of form can be impressed upon original substance without causing the creation of the form. – Wallace D Wattles	
F.E.A.R	103
Fear is only the absence of love, just as darkness is the absence of light. – Eric Pearl	
Process is Progress	107
The important thing is that you move. - Solomon	
PART 4 – My Analysis Thus Far	115
We Are Individuals Working in Harmony Together	116
Everybody's individual existence is a symphony. – Solomon	
You Are the Sun	131
Rediscover you. – Joanne Ong	
References	134
Acknowledgements	137
About the Author	139

INTRODUCTION

This is a manuscript. This is my life's manuscript thus far. It's forever growing; forever changing. I prefer calling it a manuscript because I like to see myself as a composer, creating a harmonious symphony with the instruments which I can call up at my will. My manuscript is my creative field. My music theory, like the laws of the universe, is the basis of my masterpiece. Hearing the piece in my head, feeling the emotions in my soul, I begin to write out my masterpiece, utilising the rhythm, melody and harmonies created by the instruments in my head and re-creating it on the paper before me. There will be times when I find myself stuck, out of "creative juices" or simply frustrated. Those are the times when I realise that I just need some time out to myself, to gather my thoughts and listen to my instincts, and I will find that my music will flow again. Other times, I find that the harmonisation on my paper is not reflective of what I wanted to create in my mind, so I work at it again and again, until the desired result is achieved.

My intent here is to continue to grow for as long as I live. I am a work in progress. I am never "finished". There are always new "things" for me to discover. Even as I return to my older materials and I re-read them again, I'd pick up something new at each stage of my growth. Solomon, from "Solomon Speaks on Reconnecting Your Life" by Eric Pearl and Frederick Ponzlov, calls it *transition* from one phase to another.

The idea for this manuscript began as my way of sorting out my life thus far. To sort through what has happened up until this point; what I have learnt up until now.

I may also give this manuscript for my children later on in life: when they are older and start to ask the questions of *Who am I? Why am I here? What is my life purpose? How does the universe work? Why?*

I have never received satisfactory answers to the above questions. Hence, I made it my quest to find out. I hope that my search will yield the results to help my children grow up "faster", so that they can proceed on their quest in this lifetime quicker than me. In essence, I want to "bring them up to speed" quicker so that they can go on to help others, and elevate the planet's vibration (which was the message that came to me very strongly when I had "The Reconnection" done back in 2010).

My original thoughts were never on publishing my manuscript. Then, one day I realised something. What would happen if I do publish it? What if I can help someone else in the process? What if I can reach out to other souls beyond those whom I come face to face with in this lifetime? I would be reaching out to the souls who are calling out for help: the souls who require that spark of light in their hearts to set their heart on fire. And then, these souls will proceed on their journey, and continue to help those whom they can reach. It's a ripple effect. I may have to put my vulnerability on display, but I have to start somewhere. Besides, Dr Brené Brown, the author of numerous books including "The Power of Vulnerability" doesn't think that vulnerability is a weakness; she sees it as a power to help one go through their life:

> *Owning our story can be hard but not nearly as difficult as spending our lives running from it. Embracing our vulnerabilities is risky but not nearly as dangerous as giving up on love and belonging and joy – the experiences that make us the most vulnerable. Only when we are brave enough to explore the darkness will we discover the infinite power of our light... Vulnerability is the birthplace of innovation, creativity and change.*

There is power in sharing our stories. We all live different lives and have different perspectives in life. Sharing our stories help us to understand ourselves and each other on a greater scale so that we can help one another understand and move through life, with love, joy and gratitude in all that we do.

FOREWORD

The Sun Within is a great book to reflect on where you are with your personal life journey and for those interested in understanding themselves better. Joanne Ong encouragingly teaches us to be whole individually, to be connected spiritually with one another, and to trust in the process that will lead to growth, healing and development. This book will show you how the greatest difficulties also provide the greatest opportunities for growth, new awareness, and a deeper connection with ourselves, with others, and with life itself.

Joanne communicates in a clear, articulate, authentic, down-to-earth, and easily-to-digest manner. This book has given me insight and answers that have helped me tremendously with my own awakening. Joanne makes you think about life in a way that puts everything in a different perspective. Once you learn to look at your life and situations differently, you begin to enjoy more and realize what a gift every day is.

Joanne's poetic exploration of who we are in the world we live in is filled with a clarity and beauty beyond any other work I have come across. She goes beneath the surface, exposing the fear that prevents most of us from moving forward. You have a place and a purpose, and its up to you to find out what that is.

> *"Once we know what our life purpose is, as well as what our fears are, we work towards our vision of our purpose, conquering our fears and growing spiritually as we do so."* – Joanne Ong

Since we are on a constant quest to better ourselves and our lives, The Sun Within empowers you to do what you must in order to be your best you. It illuminates your commitment to your goals, which ultimately will lead to you doing or being anything your heart desires. Sometimes we get so caught up in our goals and where we want to be that we lose the ability to enjoy what we have; this can lead to never truly being satisfied with life.

When I realized the shift needed to be made within me for me to be okay with my life, I let go of all the troubling things in my life that are beyond my control and just focused on improving myself.

No one else controls how you feel; you're no longer an emotional puppet on the string of everyone else's behavior, attitudes, decisions, choices, etc. You can feel inner joy/peace no matter what.

This book has some marvelous insights into self-actualization that really resonate with me, and are entirely congruent with my own experiences. It is about using our everyday events to learn to let go and accept what is happening in our lives and use that for spiritual growth. It forces all of us to take personal responsibility or our own actions.

I have learned that I need to forget about all the troubling things in my life that are beyond my control and just focus on improving myself. We are a product of our environment and to shift our core beliefs is extremely difficult. Joanne provides us with the steps we need to take. As time passes and knowledge accumulates, what you once learned may no longer work; changing yourself can be quite a challenge. Joanne has an uncanny insight into any human's ingrained habits and found inspirational ways to identify and then transform them.

We all really need to open our minds and listen to the truth. Oftentimes the most transforming moments occur in the most everyday situations. Joanne provided a spiritual framework for me to understand my behavior and place it into context. This book has helped me be more positive and more grateful for what exists right around me now.

This book goes so deep into connecting with your inner soul that I could literally feel the energy of what the words were saying. I now can relate what I'm learning and reading to everyday life. In a simple, easily understood manner, many issues that had been limiting me were laid out.

The end goal here is that amidst the spiritual undertones of the book, what Joanne is really educating people about is self-awareness, which is the cornerstone of growing emotional intelligence.

So, if you are looking for ways to make yourself a better person, look no further than within.

    Judy O'Beirn
    International Bestselling Author of *Unwavering Strength* series

PART 1

Who Am I? My Journey So Far

WHO AM I?

I am sure I have asked my mum when I was young. I am sure I have asked myself throughout my influential teenage years. I normally find myself asking the question whenever something really good or something bad has happened to me.

Who am I?

I remember asking my mum that question when I was about three or so. Mum told me that I am my name, followed by, "That's a stupid question!"

When I asked myself the same question in my teenage years, usually after I'd done really badly in a test or an exam, I would come up with self-destructive responses like, "You're stupid!", " You're useless!" or "You can't even do this!"

Adulthood was much the same whenever something embarrassing or bad happened to me. I'd repeat that mantra that I had since I was a teenager. When something really good happened to me, I wouldn't be able to answer that, except to say that "I'm me!"

Bob Proctor, a world-renowned mentor, coach, teacher and expert on the human mind and potential, tells us that we're not our name. He says:

> *We are spiritual beings having a physical experience. We're gifted with an intellect, and spirit is always for expansion and fuller expression. We want to stretch. We need to stretch.*

WHY AM I HERE?

Solomon (from "Solomon Speaks on Reconnecting Your Life" by Eric Pearl and Frederick Ponzlov) says:

> *We were put on this planet to experience joy. To understand the beauty, the depth, the excitement of the life experience. To thoroughly embody it, to become joyful in it, and by doing so, become compassionate with other people.*
>
> *You are here because you are a part of a greater sphere in this plane. You have an energy that has sprung from the well of existence. It is here to manifest in this plane. You are here to understand That Which Is… You are here for your own endowment. There is greatness within all that needs to be released.*

Solomon talks about soul reincarnation, volunteering to be there for another soul to learn: *Volunteer to be the four-year-old to walk in front of that truck.*

If it is true that we all have soul contracts, then does that not mean that everything has already been predetermined? If that is the case, does that mean that we have no choice in this world? Are we here to experience everything that we're experiencing, good or bad? Is that it?

My instinct told me there is more and a deeper meaning to life than predetermined forces and events. I have been told over and over again: you have choices to make. Your choice will determine the path you take. This goes against the predetermined idea, so I had to investigate further.

As I searched, I came across Bob Proctor's material. Another interesting concept caught my attention. Paradigms. In Bob's words:

> *Paradigms are a multitude of habits that guide every move you make. They affect the way you eat, the way you walk, even the way you talk.*

They govern your communication, your work habits, your successes and your failures.

For the most part, your paradigms didn't originate with you. They're the accumulated inheritance of other people's habits, opinions, and belief systems. Yet they remain the guiding force in YOUR life.

Negative and faulty paradigms are why ninety-some percent of the population keeps getting the same results, year in and year out.

Bob says that we have been programmed in our ways since we were children. If that is the case, and since I believe in reincarnation, I have no doubt that our paradigms do contribute towards our spiritual growth.

RELIGION AND SPIRITUALITY

I believe in reincarnation. I believe in soul contracts. I believe that many of the things which happened when we are really young, and some of the people whom we come to meet in our lives have been predetermined before our birth. We predetermine what it is that we want to experience and grow from BEFORE we come into this world, into this plane of existence. And our choices affect our spiritual growth later on in life.

In my case, I had chosen to come into a South-East Asian family with a mix of religious backgrounds. Although my parents called themselves Buddhists, they were not your typical idea of Buddhists who sit, meditate and chant. As the oldest child of two, I remember going to Chinese temples which practiced polytheism when I was young. We would be taken to these temples where a special person would go into a trance and start doing things like sitting on a bed of nails and take on a male's voice (if the person is a female), convey the messages required, scribble a "fu" or a protective talisman on a yellow sheet of rice paper, fold it, and give it to Mum who then burns the talisman, puts it in water and gives it to us to drink to protect us. There are numerous deities all around the temples; they all have their own special place and corners. I remember being quite afraid of some of the deities because they did look pretty scary to me.

My paternal side of the family was either Chinese polytheist or Buddhists. My maternal side consists of 2 aunties who are Catholics (one converted by choice, the other through marriage) and another is a Muslim (converted through marriage). It may be hard to imagine in the Western world today, but all my aunts and my mum are as close as can be. In fact, my aunties would even discuss the Quran and the Bible and comment on the similarities within the 2 books. My Buddhist maternal grandparents lived with my Catholic aunts and uncle until they passed over.

Mum and dad were not strict with our religious teaching. We were not regular temple visitors. I have attended church functions. I have attended Islamic functions. I have been to Buddhist rituals. I was at my grandparents' funerals where the traditional Chinese culture was to burn incense, paper cars/maids/butlers/clothes/houses/silver/gold: believing that those who have passed over will have a comfortable life "on the other side". The annual "Qing Ming" was to celebrate those souls who have passed on by making offerings to them.

My childhood world on spirituality was very open and it allowed me to be open minded to anything and everything that was made available to me. Since I was young, I was brought up to believe in mediums who speak to those who have passed on and in psychics who can foretell the future. I was taught that I have past lives which I have to deal with (hence, reincarnation). I've been brought up to believe that there are people who can see and hear spirits when normal people can't see them.

I recall being brought up in a rather superstitious family. I wasn't allowed to blow a musical instrument or whistle at night. I wasn't allowed to cut my nails, wash my hair or sweep the floor on the first day of Chinese New Year. In addition to that, I was taught to have a full container of rice for the new year, have leftover rice and fish from the night before in order to usher in the new year. I was brought up to believe in Feng Shui and was not allowed to point at the moon (or I may get my ears cut off). All these superstitions and traditions became a part of me, some of which I carried forth into my adulthood.

I feel that it is the correct choice for me as this "loose reign" on religion and spirituality allowed me to delve further into the world beyond what we can see. I still recall the dreams that I had as a child; and these dreams came true years later, just like déjà vu.

As I grew up, I paid less attention to this side of me, but in the back of my mind, the belief is always there. I was able to see, hear and feel spirits (sometimes) just "out of nowhere". An example is when I literally saw sparks of lights in my daughter's room when she was about one-year old when I had asked for help to calm down her immense screaming. I saw the sparks of light and she went from standing and screaming in her cot to lying down on herself, and sobbing herself to sleep almost straight away (and there was literally no other physical being in the room!). Another example was when someone whispered in my ear to email my best friend in Malaysia. I thought it was a strange request, but I did anyway. That's when she emailed me to tell me that she had just gone through a major turning point in her life and broke up with her long term boyfriend!

I would say that the one course which truly opened up my awareness was the Reconnective Healing seminar I attended in July 2016. As I have discovered, what normally happens just prior to my Reconnective Healing sessions, things just seem to "fall into place" the moment I decided to take on the course. I started reading materials which I thought were unrelated to the course, as a form of self-growth. When I attended the course, it was as if the dots were being connected together, albeit, the dots were still far apart. The course talked about being "in the moment", and explained what quantum physics have been trying to ascertain thus far. However, what really got my attention was the obliteration of our human sense of space and time; our sense of being multidimensional beings. What I learnt through holographic and distance healings reinforced the connection that we are all in essence, one. We are all a part of the one universe and we are all interconnected.

As it happens, I finished reading Anita Moorjani's "Dying to be Me" on the plane, on way back from my course and it all started making sense to me. It was as if her book gave me the "in-between" dots which I tried to connect at the seminar. It gave me my "Aha!" moment and everything started to make sense from there on. Finally, I understood that we are all a part of one universe. There is no "us and them": there is only us, there is only one. I've finally figured out that we have come onto this plane with physical boundaries to assist us in our experience, but in essence, the physical boundaries merely help us to live from a single point of view. To access true healing, which is healing beyond the physical, we need to realise that we are all interconnected, that there are no boundaries in an infinite universe, and that we can heal one another via our intention to help the other person.

"Solomon Speaks" and "Dying to be me" gave me the confidence to continue to trust in my own instincts. Bob Proctor's online courses and live streams (which were more on a conscious level) taught me the exact same thing. I'm still learning to trust my instincts more, as I feel that it is part of my growth to be able to follow my heart which should lead me to what I need to do in this lifetime to fulfill my preconceived mission on this plane. I can only learn to trust myself more and more as time goes on, to realise what Solomon has been saying all along: that I am enough.

ENERGY

I remember as a young child of about 2 or 3, I would draw circles around my heart and my third eye area. I still have the vivid image in my mind. I was lying down on the couch in the living room. There was no TV there. And I started playing with my hands and would feel this energy between them. Then I started to draw circles and I could feel that on the other hand even though they're weren't touching. I continued to play with my heart and my forehead, and I could feel those areas vibrating, pulsating through.

I must have really done something because I remember calling out to Mum and told her I was feeling very "funny". Mum would ask me, "What do you mean by funny?" I couldn't explain it so I showed her what I was doing. She just told me to stop doing that and to stop being silly.

To be honest, that was probably the last time I really tried to play with my own energy. Until I rediscovered it later on in adulthood, after a series of events.

My belief that "there is something greater in the universe" had led me to books and materials on energetic healing and aura reading. I still recall the first time I saw my own aura on my hands and in the mirror. As I relaxed my eyes, concentrating on a point just between my fingers and just above my head, I began to see a bright white light forming around the boundaries of my fingers and my head. As I continued to relax, I saw a blue light emanating from the white light. It was so surreal, seeing my fingers and my reflection and white and blue lights coming out of it. The colours were intense, but they were not solid like a wall. The colours moved with me as I moved my fingers and my head. I was perplexed: shocked yet happy that I could see it with my own eyes! I've also been able to see blue lights from time to time ever since then. It's a reassurance for me that I'm being guided, on the right path, and that I'm not alone.

I was also interested in and attempted energetic healings such as reiki. However, I found it quite cumbersome that there are so many pre-ordained procedures that I have to do before and after the healings. I didn't like the idea that a "master" has more power and one has to be "inducted" to be involved in the process. It just didn't sit right with me.

When my son was diagnosed with Juvenile Dermatomyositis (a rare auto-immune disease that affects 3 in a million children with no known causes and no cure), that was a turning point for me. Before his diagnosis, no one could tell us exactly what he had (and he couldn't speak back then since he was less than two years old at that time). As I continued on my research, I remember asking for help, saying, "Please show me exactly what he has." I almost gave up at that point, but something within me told me to search once again. I followed my instincts on the search terms. I found two articles which were of interest to me. I clicked on both. One page never loaded. The other was the exact article with the blood test results, photos of his symptoms and treatment methodologies-a medical article which was published in a pediatric journal.

My son was slowly recovering, but something in me told me to search for more. I came across Reconnective Healing and met a lovely lady, Jacqui, who was willing to work on the both of us since I still had to hold and be with him for the sessions. Anyone who has worked or been involved with Reconnective Healing would tell you that the healing does not come with a set of expected results:

> *Your healing may come in the form you anticipate... Or it may come in a form you haven't even dreamed of, one that the universe has designed specifically for you. Healings can come in all forms. The best way to allow for a healing is to proceed in a state of expectancy, without specific expectations or attachment to results. – Eric Pearl*

Did the healing help my son? I don't know. His condition didn't suddenly go into remission, as per my original expectations (or should I say wanting). However, the dull backache that I had for 2 years had suddenly disappeared after just one session! So I'm sure it did help him, in some way or another.

SOUL CONTRACTS

We find "ourselves" in interaction with others. - Solomon

You have been here innumerable times. You're here because your energy draws you together. Your life is of a greater sphere of influence than you are presently aware. It is coming to you on a different plane, and will be unveiled to you as your progress continues forward. Your mission comes in interaction (with others), not isolation. Your definition of your life is in your ability to open it to others. That is what allows greatness to enter into your soul. – Solomon

I find this to be a very intricate process: one that requires such precision that a slight movement in the time frame would make it impossible for us to be where we are today.

The more I look at my soul contracts up until this point, the more I see the predetermined paths I had made prior to being born onto this plane. I believe that we cross paths with those whom we are close to (or were close to) by virtue of timing and for good reasons. We need to make the most of these "meetings" and "events" and learn from them the best that we can.

I was an overdue baby. I was supposed to have been born about a week beforehand. It's New Year's Day. My mother had a severe back pain but being New Year's Day, there were no experienced obstetricians or nurses around. The on-duty nurse massaged her back, having no idea that she was in labour at that time. When the obstetrician finally came the next day and asked how mum was, she said she was fine. When asked if I was still kicking, Mum said, "No." She scheduled an emergency caesarean for Mum that day, and when I was born, I was blue/black in colour. I was rushed to the incubator where I remained for two weeks before I was allowed to go home.

Being born a day later also meant that I had missed the cut-off date for schooling by a whole year. The schooling system was so strict that no matter how academically or socially capable I was, there was no way they would skip me by one year in school. So I was basically held back for an entire year.

I met my husband at university. We were doing the same course in first year and shared many classes together. He, too, almost didn't make it into university that year. He required special permission to leave national service three months earlier, and was almost not accepted into the university because his application was made after the closing date.

Add to that the fact that all I had ever wanted to do when I was in high school was Medicine. The year that I applied for it was the first year where they introduced the Undergraduate Medical Admissions Test (UMAT). I had no idea what it was all about so I walked blindly into the three-hour exam and walked out "floating", not knowing what had just happened. I found out I failed miserably in the exam just one week before my Tertiary Entrance Examination. I had to remove Medicine as my first preference and change my preference to Engineering and Commerce instead. I got in to my chosen course, and the rest was history.

When we started to get to know one another, we had a very strange feeling which we couldn't explain. Even though we had only known each other for a few months, we felt like we'd known each other for years. It was as if we had known each other from a previous life. Being together as friends, we felt alive and vibrant. But when we were apart for a week whilst we were on "trial" to see if we could be separated, we both felt lost and awkward. That trial made me think really hard: *should I follow my head or my heart?*

The day finally came when he actually "asked me out." He knew he was taking his chances with me when he did it: after all, I was supposed to be "going out" with someone else at that time, someone whom I had a crush on for years back in high school, but only gathered the courage to ask him out in our first year at university.

I still remember very vividly our surroundings when he asked me out. I knew this day would come. I knew I had to make a choice. I tossed and turn in the few nights before, constantly asking myself, "Should I follow my head? Or should I follow my heart? I have known my 'current boyfriend' for years, since high school, whereas I only know this other person for a few months! This is crazy!" My head kept telling me to stick with the "safe side," with the person whom I've known for years but my heart was telling me that something in that relationship would not work out. My head and my heart had constant arguments, up until this moment where he (my husband) is on my bed, and just asked me out. He squeezed my talking Tweety bird: "I wonder what dat puddy tat is up to?!" There was a pause. My gut and my heart took over my head. I leaned over for our very first kiss. I could feel his heartbeat, and mine, together. He squeezed Tweety bird again and this time it said, "I wuv you."

And I've never regretted following my heart since then…

Another soul contract would be with my parents. What made their marriage different was the fact that my father had spent most of his time (almost 20 years in fact) working away from the family. When we were young, he would take the bus and return every weekend to see us, then take the overnight bus to go to work again on the same day. When we had moved to Australia, and dad returned to work in Singapore, we only saw him about 4 times a year, and for about 3 to 4 days each time. My mother was alone most of the time, looking after both my brother and I whilst she worked full time. In fact, at one point, she was even working two jobs so I had learned to do all the housework from an early age. As soon as I had my driver's license, I would help her buy the weekly groceries and learnt how to budget and stretch the money.

Most of the women whom I know cannot even survive at home without their partners or husband. They would tell me how stressed they are with their children whenever their partners aren't around to help. My husband got a job which involved a lot of travelling all around the world, but I didn't complain. I just looked back at what mum and dad used to do and I coped. My husband used to travel for work whilst I was pregnant and when I had a baby or a toddler to look after and I thought nothing of it. If my mum could do it, so could I.

I've been told by different psychics that my daughter is going to be a special being who is going to be a "teacher" to the world and help a lot of people. If that is true, then home and family influence would be vital in her upbringing. How can I teach her to reach for her soul purpose if I do not know how to do it myself? The answer: I need to do it. I need to be able to look for it. Find it. Find my soul purpose. Find out what I'm here to do. I need to be a model for her to teach her that it is possible to succeed in life, doing what one loves to do.

No psychic ever mentioned my son's condition. I feel that it was deliberate that they were never shown this. If I were ever told that he'd have an incurable disease, I know I'd panic and our life course may be different to the one I'm on now. So what has my son's condition taught me? He has awakened me to the awareness within me. I am stronger, more open minded and more capable (spiritually, mentally and physically) because of him. He also taught me a very important lesson: family. Before he was diagnosed, I had mapped out plans of what my husband and I needed to do to build our wealth. I was very materialistic. In some ways, I became like my father and I was willing to do things like leave them for a while whilst I worked. My children were not my core focus: my core focus was earning money to provide the "desired lifestyle" for us all. It was either or. I was certain I couldn't have both.

Then he fell sick. Very sick in about three to four months. He couldn't turn in bed. He couldn't pick himself up. He was choking on his own saliva. He was ulcerated inside and outside. And the worst thing was that no one could tell us why. And after he was diagnosed, we were told there was no cure. We could only hope that it goes into permanent remission.

Our hospital appointments and interviews with registrars/medicine students at hospital (he was always "exhibit A" because he's such a "rare case") made me realise that an abundance in wealth isn't everything. What is the point in having all the wealth if you do not get to spend it with the ones whom you love? I hit a turning point, thanks to my son's condition. I am forever grateful to him for showing me that there is more to life than being materialistic in this world. That health and family are all integral to one's spiritual growth. Somehow, we must reach a balance and be able to juggle all these in the air without dropping them.

On the surface, it may not appear to be much. However, if we truly look for it, I believe that we know the people that we do for a reason. I found that my ex-boyfriends (or those whom I had said no to) found God after their disappointment with me, and met their future partners at the churches that they attended. My brother taught me that only people who are willing and open to change can be influenced to do so. Otherwise, I would be seen a preaching and I personally dislike people who preach and tell me how to think (one of the reasons why I couldn't attend church on a regular basis, or any formal religion for that matter). My father-in-law taught me that nothing is impossible so long as you are persistent and have faith in what you do. My mother-in-law taught me how to handle criticism in my life. I have a variety of friends and colleagues-from open-minded, self-aware friends to those who are very much on the conscious plane and do not believe in God or in the universe. I see how their beliefs about themselves affect who they have become; how things have or have not worked out for them. Generalisations cannot be made either: I work in an engineering environment with some who are so closed minded that they do not even believe in alternative medicine like chiropractic and acupuncture, to those who were willing to let me help them heal with Reconnective Healing.

We are all here and know one another for a reason. Question is: are you willing to take a look at your contracts and learn from it? Who and why have people come and gone in your life? What have they taught you?

THE RECONNECTION AND ENERGETIC ATTRACTIONS

It was because of my son that I had "The Reconnection" done. Before he had his condition, I would have never even contemplated or found this alternative healing method.

For those who are unfamiliar with it, you can search for it on www.thereconnection.com where you will find the difference between Reconnective Healing and The Reconnection. Reconnective Healing is essentially a reactivation of the healing ability within all of us, returning us to the optimal state of balance. The Reconnection, on the other hand, is only done once in your lifetime, over a two-day period, and facilitates an exchange of the Reconnective Healing frequencies to help accelerate you onto your life path. The first day is where your energy is opened up to allowing the frequencies to flow through you, and the second day is when your energy is sealed up once again. It was only years later that I found out that other practitioners have also experienced unexplainable electrical disturbances when they come into contact with the frequencies.

The moment I made the decision to have The Reconnection done in 2008, and made the appointment with Jacqui, things just fell into place. I wanted a makeover for myself to start anew after my son's diagnosis. I booked a photoshoot with a photographer that I was drawn to for some reason. The appointment was made, and I took my annual leave to do the photoshoot. However, no one was there. I called after a while of waiting and the photographer spoke to me the whole time whilst he drove to the studio. Since there was no one else there, he did my makeup and styling. As he did, we continued to chat. It turned out that he was also an NLP coach. All the while, he instilled positive, uplifting messages into me during the makeup and photo session. All the messages from my "A Star Student Course" which I took when I was still in primary school came flooding back to me: power of positivity, self-belief, and goal-setting.

Prior to The Reconnection, I kept seeing 333 everywhere I went. During the first session, the CD player refused to play several minutes into the session. I felt my awareness opening up through my "third eye". I also heard voices telling me that I'm helping to elevate the planet's vibration and helping my children to do the same. Uplifting positive songs came on air as I drove home. I changed the frequency in my daughter's room just by going into her room. We had a baby monitor in her room and it registered a different frequency even after I had left the room. I reached Jacqui's house the next day for session two (it needed to be done over 2 consecutive days) at the exact same time. This time, I felt as if she was removing nails from my feet because they were so sore that I couldn't help but grunt. Jacqui said her hands had never pulsated so much in all The Reconnections that she has performed over the years. She told me she was sure that I was destined to help others heal.

How was I going to help others to heal? What do you mean by healing? I had no idea. But as I found out later, the moment I decide to do something that is in line with my soul purpose, it is as if the universe delivers everything to me very quickly and at the exact right moment.

LISTEN TO YOUR INSTINCT

Hear your own music. - Solomon

There have been many instances where I have refused to listen to my instinct, to that *little* voice inside of me. And I got into all sorts of issues as a result of that.

After the labour pain that I went through with my first-born, I decided that there had to be a better way for childbirth. Halfway through my second pregnancy, I discovered hypnobirthing through my research online and took on board the idea. My body aches were relieved during the nights as I practiced it, and I still vividly recall the midwife telling my husband, "That must be some music that she's listening to. I've never seen anyone so calm in a labour ward before!" and I could hear my husband smile back at her. The result was a very alert baby and mum at the end of week-long labour and 8.5 hours of induction.

Sometimes, we work our body through so much that it cannot handle it further and it turns into a dis-ease. I was admitted into emergency several years ago where I had severe pain near my appendix area and couldn't even walk. The doctors conducted blood tests and scans and found nothing but told me that I needed my appendix removed. I refused to believe them as a little voice inside of me told me that I did not have appendicitis. I listened to my instinct again which told me that I wasn't respecting my feminine side and that I needed to reach a balance. I left hospital that same day and I never had any problem with the area since that day.

Prior to my son's diagnosis, we were told that he had a dermatology issue. We had asked to see a specific dermatologist but were told we had to wait for four months. In the four months, his condition deteriorated significantly. We went to another doctor where we asked for blood tests to be done.

Unfortunately, blood tests showed nothing unusual because the ordered tests were not the ones required for the diagnosis. Something told me to dig deeper. That's when I came across the article in a paediatric journal online. On the day he was admitted into hospital, he was tended to by one of the few Juvenile Dermatomyositis specialists in the world straightaway and has since been under his care.

I'm not advocating against going to the doctor. I'm just saying that sometimes, one needs to listen to his/her own intuition if what you're being told doesn't feel right. If something isn't working for you, listen to your body. Pay attention to your instincts. Act on your instincts. It may put you in the right direction or at least steer you to the path that you're supposed to be on. It certainly saved my son's life.

Quote from Solomon Speaks, Chapter 7:

> *Do not look outside yourself for answers. All you need to change is to learn to listen to your instinct. Allow your instinct to lead you. You are grasping at a great many ideas that are outside of you. The ideas have merit, but the only real ideas that have merit for you are those that come from inside you.*
>
> *The real flow of energy will feel positive in your life. You will feel heightened by it. You will feel more alive. It's trial and error with you, because you're a specific instrument. You have to learn how to play yourself. No one has printed books on how to play you. Hear your own music.*
>
> *Act from your heart. It will come in a greater space as soon as you allow yourself to be healed internally.*

PERSONALITY – CHILDHOOD

There comes a transition in children's lives where they have to abandon that (greater self) knowledge and root themselves in this plane. Much is lost so that much can be learned, and then re-accessed later in life. But in order for them to really understand the lessons in this place, they have to let go of the encyclopedia they brought with them. It's a closed-book test. I think you might want to look at that transition. – Solomon

My recollection of my childhood stems all the way back to when I was very young. I was rather boisterous, vocal and bossy, even if I was the youngest in the group. There would be times where I disagreed with the "leader of the pack", and I would argue my point. Others would then listen to me and we'd play it my way. Or, we would change the rules to suit us all. I was open to change.

Primary school was much the same for me. I wasn't afraid of responsibility or being picked as a leader for anything that came my way. I would take part in all the extra-curricular activities that I could handle. If I saw someone being treated unfairly, I'd stand up for that person.

My earliest exposure to the law of attraction was through Dr Lawrence Walter Ng's "A Star Student" course. I was impressed by how the course was delivered with such energy and liveliness. Up until today, I still use some of the content taught, including speed reading, photographic memory and goal setting. The course was moulded to suit younger children and as I look back now, I'm quite impressed at how we were taught to be caring, that we were enough, how to see us achieving our goals in our minds and pushing our boundaries to reach those goals. He taught us about the conscious and the subconscious minds and how to reprogram ourselves to a higher level of thinking.

Those were very powerful and important lessons. I sometimes wonder how many of us "graduates" of the "A Star Student" course actually continued to practise these principles in their lives. I've certainly forgotten about these until I met my photographer several years ago; then all such memories and ideas started flooding back to me. The more I take on board the ideas of the law of attraction now, the more reading materials and books I attract into my life. And the more that I read, the more that I practice this and find that it worked.

When I first started my manifestations, my husband was sceptical to begin with, but he never discouraged me from doing so. Instead, he did the opposite and I ended up treating it as a game. Through my manifestations, I learnt that I am capable of getting what I want in life. And I have my husband to thank for that.

The primary law of vibration and secondary law of attraction has worked so well for me that I have attracted things into my life that I've never dreamt of owning. I started with small items like a specific model of watch or jewellery. As I progressed, I went on to bigger things like attracting our dream home in the location that I wanted with the features that I was looking for. I've manifested buying a car and the exact amount that I would write on the cheque. I've manifested holidays which I didn't know how they would happen but they did. The one common theme I found in my manifestations was that I had faith that they would happen. I didn't know how, but I assured my husband that they would happen-and they did. Napoleon Hill, the author of "Think and Grow Rich" was right: *The starting point of all achievement is desire and there are no limitations to the mind except those we acknowledge.*

I did have limitations to my manifestation though. I found it very hard to attract lottery winnings (just like most people in the world). I believe that the reason for this is because I had come into this lifetime with a purpose: to be of service to others. I should not think of money first. Money is merely a by-product and is in direct correlation of the size of my service to others. Solomon said:

> *The matter of money is another question entirely. It may deal with your reluctance, in a way, to feel the flow of life that is around you. Your hesitancy often in the face of this force is due to your lack of understanding of your own nature as a giver and not a receiver. It's not an easy*

concept, but I can only tell you that your life force is growing and that it will continue to expand; and as it expands, it will attract to it the kind of financial support your desire. That will come first, not the other way around. The financial support will not show its face until you change your life from within. And then it will come to you. It's problematic at the moment, definitely, but your life is changing – you must feel that. And as it is changing and accepting in a larger picture your potential for growth, it will come to you; it will be part of you.

I'm always excited whenever one of my manifestations come true and I try to share my stories with others in order to encourage them to attract the good into their lives. That's when I notice two very distinct groups of people: those who believe, and those who don't. Those with a positive mental attitude, and those who are completely immersed in negativity. Those who are open-minded and positive tell me their good stories. Those who weren't didn't succeed.

PERSONALITY – ADOLESCENCE

Self-worth is the understanding that you are the universe – Solomon

Adolescence wasn't the best of my years. However, I choose to look at those years as a lesson for me. Solomon said:

> *Suffering is not necessarily something that needs to be avoided. It's incredibly beneficial if viewed in the proper perspective. And what we do is train ourselves through our spiritual paths to view this suffering in an enlightened viewpoint to see how it will make us expand our growth within the universe. Then it becomes essential; it becomes fulfilling. For the whole experience.*
>
> *The important thing is that any spiritual path opens the door and makes you able to access whatever is to come. But you have to be in that process of opening doors. Trials make us stronger.*

My parents moved to a foreign country when I was thirteen. We all had to cope with a new life, new friends: new everything.

The first high school I attended was impressed on my mind and led the way to how I lived in my adolescent years and the early years of my adulthood. My first school peers were more interested in impressing the boys than they were at studying. They were followers who believed that if you did well at school, you were a "square" (a calling they give to someone who does better at tests or exams than themselves) and it's "not cool" to be a square. They also told me that I had a "funny" accent.

Naturally, as an adolescent who was trying desperately to fit into the new environment, I adopted their thoughts and behaviour, hoping that I would be a part of them. But no matter what I did, they still called me a square and didn't take on any of my suggestions to join extra-curricular activities at school.

When we moved house, I moved to another school. I learnt from my first school that I should not portray who I can be as I would then be called names. However, I must have absorbed so much that my new friends at school didn't even realise that I had only been in Australia for 4 months. I no longer had a "funny accent" and I learnt to keep everything to myself so that no one would know how I'd done in tests and exams. I no longer suggested attending extra-curricular activities because I knew it would be seen as being "uncool". I ended up like everyone else around me. A follower. I conformed to what society expected of me.

Bob was right when he said that anxiety is suppressed, not expressed. I had everything bottled up within me and I ended up becoming a shy, introverted and fearful follower: the complete opposite to my childhood personality.

This went on for years. Negativity came and spiralled me downwards. I was always anxious of what others thought of me. I was afraid to ask questions (in case people thought I was dumb). I had repressed so much within me that I started believing that I was a failure. My environment was reflective of my thoughts. I started doing badly in tests and exams and couldn't really see how I could improve on my scores. I spiralled down so much and became so angry that I would sometimes take a pen or pencil and snap it in half with my bare hands. I would then start taking the sharp end of the broken pen to start scratching/cutting my arm, my wrist, my hands. Looking back now, I was in a dangerous state but no one knew about it: not until one of my closer friends started noticing some scars and marks on my arms. But even they couldn't talk me out of my situation. I had buried myself so deep that I couldn't "dig myself out again".

The self-harm continued into my university years. I would either try to cut myself or hit my head on my metal bed head or pound my hands against the table and wall or slap myself until I turned red. I needed marks to show on my body to show others that I've been trying to hurt myself. I needed to externally vent my internal frustration because I could no longer withhold it within me. The marks were to show my invisible anger and uselessness in a physical form. When I saw the marks, it validated my "uselessness" and the vicious cycle continued.

The only person who stopped me from self-harm was my (now) husband. He saw the marks. He saw what I was doing to myself and he stopped me by convincing me over time that my self-harm was doing nothing except damaging my own self-belief and self-worth. He was right.

I took a turn since meeting my husband. He made me believe in myself again. He brought me out from within: the real me that I had suppressed for so many years. I slowly regained my confidence, strength and leadership. When things didn't work out well, he taught me about perception. We can always see a glass as either half full or half empty. An important lesson he taught me was not to be petty with money, to ignore (non-constructive) criticism of myself and to speak my mind. If I didn't agree with something, I was allowed to voice my opinion, and it's exactly just that: an opinion. Everyone's entitled to their own opinions, whether they're right or wrong.

Solomon says:

> *Problems are not problems- they are lessons to be learned. Growth waiting to happen. Cutting yourself off from the growth is regression, isolation. You must embrace your difficulty and rejoice in it. Because it will catapult you to greater victories to come.*

SYNCHRONICITIES AND DETOURS

When your desires are strong enough, you will appear to possess super-human powers to achieve it – Napoleon Hill

Your energy is of a greater life force that is coming through you. Your thoughts are your energy manifest. It will lead you to your instinct. Your instinct is the sum total of your lives' experience. It is the encyclopedia of humanity – Solomon

My husband and I got engaged just before we started working as graduate engineers and planned to get married as soon as we could. We planned to buy or build a house together with whatever money that we had as a deposit prior to getting married. And we did. Despite the fact that I was working 500km away (5 hours by car, 6 hours by bus each way), I returned home every Friday evening, so that I could continue to teach piano and organ on Saturdays and Sundays. I would leave on Sunday afternoons to start work again on Mondays. It reminded me of the years when my father left us in Malaysia whilst he worked in Singapore, catching a bus back every Friday night to see us, and then leaving every Sunday for work again.

In between my music teaching, we would go house hunting. When we couldn't find one that we could agree on, I started looking at land so that we could build what we wanted. I found a piece of land in the papers way above what we could afford. Nonetheless, we checked it out. We drove around the neighbourhood and found one that was similar in size and shape just on the street behind the one that was advertised in the papers. It wasn't advertised anywhere and my husband had to go through a few numbers to get through to the agent before making an offer on it. We paid less than the asking price of the original block of land that we had been looking at.

Some people say that detours tend to make you learn. In this case, the detour was literally what we needed to find what we wanted.

When we first looked at investment properties several years later, I found a rear block of land in a decent suburb and almost made an offer on it. We researched further and found out that the construction cost would be much higher and that the council's regulations were restrictive in terms of how we could build on it. Couple that with the fact that the owners declined our offer, we decided to look elsewhere for an investment property. I found our investment property a few months later in a nicer area, secured compound, closer proximity to the river and higher (and immediate) rental yield. We purchased that one instead and I found out that the original block that we had put in an offer for was now asking for a lower price than what we had originally offered.

A similar thing happened when I was looking for our next home. When I thought I found one, I rang up the agent but it took several tries to get through to him. Finally, when he returned my call, I arranged for an inspection whilst my husband was overseas at the time. I should have seen the signs around me. I arrived on time but the agent arrived late. There was a major thunderstorm that day and there was no power to the house as I inspected the house. I still called the agent over and tried to put in an offer. Upon telling him our offer, the agent refused to write it down, packed his bag and left our house. A few months down the road, I found that the asking price for that house was lower than our original offer – the one that the agent refused to write.

By then, I had found another block which I thought was perfect for us. I found a buyer's agent and got her to contact the owner. After several months, the agent finally managed to contact the owner but found out that he wanted an offer that was more than 50% of what we were willing to pay for it. I told the universe, "Thank you very much. Please show us something within our budget."

By *luck*, I came across a block just by browsing a particular agent's website which was *perfect*. The day I went to check out the block, it was a clear blue sky, 24 degrees Celsius with clear blue water and boats on the river as we crossed the bridge. When we finally got to the block, the breeze was in my face, as if whispering to me, "Welcome Home!" I know I shouldn't buy on emotions, but this was more than that. I trusted my instinct, and we ended up with a much nicer block, in a prestigious suburb, built our first modernised custom home with unobstructed views of the river and sea. Somehow, things just fell into place in terms of affordability, construction and financing of our dream home. I also found out later as we were building, that the original block that we had looked at was repossessed by the bank and sold for a higher price than what we would've paid for, though not as much as what the owner would've hoped for. Once again, I was thankful for what I had.

> *Our instinct is the sum total of All That Is. We clear a path. That is instinct... that is what guides us. Trusting the instinct and discovering it.*
> *– Solomon.*

Whenever we ask for something from the universe, we need to have the faith that we will receive it. As Hill said, "Faith is the visualisation of and belief in the attainment of your desires." Through my experiences, I learnt that if something doesn't seem quite right, I have to trust my instinct to lead the way whilst having faith that it will occur for me. It may be not what I think it is: it may turn out even better than I thought.

SPIRITUAL TO MANIFESTATION

You are a spiritual being, you have an intellect, and you live in a physical body. – Bob Proctor

Bob Proctor purports that we exist on three simultaneous planes of existence at any one time: our *spiritual, intellectual* and *physical* planes. What that means is that we are spiritual beings and therefore are able to tap into our infinite universal resource for anything that we so desire. We have the intellect to think and turn our ideas into its physical form to complement our physical being. Everything that is not natural in this world has been created twice: once in the mind of someone and another time in its physical form. We all have this innate ability to be able to turn our ideas into physicality; whether we do it consciously or not is another matter altogether.

Earl Nightingale, the "Dean of Personal Development" says, "We become what we think about." Everything that we have started off as an idea. As we draw on that idea, focus, internalise, feel it, see the idea within our grasp as if we already have it, we are then led the way to which the idea can be turned into its physical form. The important concept to remember though is that the thought which manifests is not only what we consciously think about, but that it also refers to what we unconsciously think about.

I've had numerous examples in my life when I have manifested things which I had only dreamt of, and have them "turn up" in my life when I wanted them to. The latest items which I had manifested were a pair of anniversary wedding bands for my husband and I. Here is how I went about getting those rings. I really wanted a pair of anniversary wedding bands because I had somehow lost my original wedding band which we exchanged on our wedding day. To begin with, I started with the idea of having a pair of new wedding bands. However, I went into the details of the wedding bands: the exact brand, model and type of bands that I was after. When I had the exact details of what I wanted, I pictured having the ring on my finger, with an immense sense of gratitude of having a pair of anniversary bands and the surprised look on my husband's face when I would have them delivered to his office. I then put it out to the universe exactly what I wanted, and the price I was willing to pay for them. Wishful thinking can only get one so far, and this is probably where I fell short with regards to manifesting my lottery winnings which never happened. When I received the hunch to start looking, I searched high and low for the wedding bands. I started querying the online shops, calling the shops in the country (which didn't stock them anywhere in the country and had to be specially ordered from overseas) but my will and determination were so strong that I refused to give up. As I was just about to give up, that's when I came across a website which stocked exactly what I wanted, sold new wedding bands, for a price that I was willing to pay. I started making enquiries and found that they could deliver it way earlier than my anniversary date (I had wanted it close to my anniversary date, for the added surprise element). Anyway, I proceeded with the idea of purchasing the rings.

All this time, I wanted the rings to be delivered about 2 months later so that they would arrive on our special date. Then, things started happening. It took some time for the person to locate the exact models and sizes that I was after. It was getting close to the date, so I paid extra for expedited shipping of the rings. The rings were shipped, but there were then delays with the customs being on strike. When we were out for dinner to celebrate our anniversary on Friday, my tracking number showed that the package finally arrived at customs on that date. So, it arrived on our anniversary date. However, I was getting concerned that he wouldn't get it until 2 weeks later as he was supposed to be flying overseas on Monday afternoon. Despite that, I continued to have faith that he would get them on time before he left. Monday morning came, and he rang me from the office at 9am to tell me my surprise had arrived at his desk. They were all packed, shiny, and new - just as I had imagined. And the surprising thing was that the website which I purchased from no longer existed after I purchased those rings (cue "Twilight Zone" music).

Think about what it is that you have attracted into your life so far, whether they'd be the people, things or results. How have you attracted the car that you really wanted into your life? Or that fridge into your home? What about the current house that you're living in? All these things are the product of our own manifestations, whether we notice them subconsciously or not.

Your thoughts are your energy manifest. – Solomon

JOANNE ONG

PART 2

What Makes Me, "Me"?

SOUL-PURPOSE

Your mission, in a way, is to connect a spiritual heart to a spiritual existence. It's not always an easy thing you undertake. But it is the quest of life. You must allow yourself a different space. It is time to feel much more. Allow this life force to pervade you. Understand your mission. Feel it in your life. It is not of notoriety; it is of immense greatness in the satisfying nature of the way it is permitted to flow. – Solomon

This is a question that most people will ask themselves as they begin their soul searching process. Why am I here? What can I do? What am I good at? What am I not good at? How do I determine my soul purpose?

Wayne Dyer's book, "Inspiration: Your Ultimate Calling" gives methods on how to discover your purpose. He refers to Pantajali's six conclusions on inspiration and describe what it feels like to return to the oneness, a return to the universe:

1. *When You Are Inspired... All Your Thoughts Break Their Bonds*

    Returning to Spirit results in a grand sense of being in tune with our uniquely Divine purpose. Just imagine being able to go on and on for hours at a time without experiencing fatigue, hunger, thirst, or mental exhaustion, all thanks to one factor: the willingness to be back in-Spirit.

2. *When You Are Inspired... Your Mind Transcends Limitations*

    ... imagine what it must feel like to have absolute faith-an inner knowing that it's impossible to fail, a complete absence of doubt concerning your ability to create anything you place your attention on... when we're inspired, we remember that God is always in us and we're always in God, so we're incapable of thinking limited thoughts. We're transcendent; we've gone beyond the world of boundaries and entered a space of creative knowing.

3. *When You Are Inspired… Your Consciousness Expands in Every Direction*

   When we're in-Spirit, every direction is possible for us at every moment because our consciousness happens within our mind… Our consciousness is in the absolute state of allowing-all resistance, in the form of thoughts, is non-existent.

4. *When You Are Inspired… You Find Yourself in a New, Great, and Wonderful World*

   We're back in vibrational alignment where limitations don't exist and there are no bonds, and we've left our body and all of its boundaries to live in an expanded consciousness in our mind. We now begin to think in terms of miracles being not only possible, but actively en route.

5. *When You Are Inspired… Dorman Forces, Faculties, and Talents Become Alive*

   …when we move into an awareness of inspiration, forces that we thought were either dead or unavailable come alive and are available for us to use to manifest our inspired desires.

6. *When You Are Inspired… You Discover Yourself to be a Greater Person by Far Than You Ever Dreamed Yourself to be.*

   The act of being inspired by some great purpose allows us to feel the essence of a spiritual being having a human experience, rather than the other way around.

For those who are able to meditate, their soul-purpose will come to light, if they ask for it. For the rest of us who cannot seem to meditate no matter what we do, it is about searching and finding what it is that we can and are willing to do (for others), which provides us with so much joy and contentment that we can continue to serve (people) without worrying (too much) about the financial consequences in our lives. "The Power of Purpose" by Les Brown is a good audiobook for those who are currently searching for their soul-purpose and have yet to find what it is that they truly want to do in this lifetime.

> *There is one quality which one must possess to win, and that is the definiteness of purpose, the knowledge of what one wants, and a burning desire to possess it. – Napoleon Hill*

Our purpose needs to be so strong that our burning desire keeps us going to obtain that purpose. It is through this burning desire, by holding on to our purpose, our dream, our goals, that we want it so badly such that nothing will stop us in our way. It is as if when life gets in the way, you move it out of the way so that you can achieve it.

> *You mustn't disavow your life in its path of learning. There are only lessons. There are no mistakes. And you will continue to have lessons. It's unending, but it will lead you to the space you need to be in. – Solomon*

We have to truly look within to find our purpose in life. We can ask others who are close to us to help give us some hints as to what we are good at, but it is up to us to determine what it is that we truly want to achieve in this lifetime.

> *Your energy is of the universe. Feel it in your life-in your life. In the force that motivates you. Feel it through your heart. It is your own by its force.*

> *It is an apparition of the force that is implied in life itself. You feel it in your moments of ecstasy and energy. It is always constant. You are inconstant. Your ability to access it is inconstant. You need to unleash your heart from your head. It is not a cerebral exercise. You won't find it that way. It's in your instinct. You must carry it in your instinct.*

> *You have to decide why you love this work. Where is it coming from? Where is this love for this work? You need to examine that with your heart. It is not about fulfilling your needs. It is about opening your life to experience. It's not there for gratification. It's there for exploration.*

> *There is nothing wrong with gratification, if it is the by-product of the work. If it is the initial goal, it is misguided. – Solomon*

Only we can tell if something rings as a harmony or a disharmony to us. It is up to us to tune our own instrument, and it is up to us to find out if we are working together in a symphony or if we are slightly off and need to re-tune ourselves to align ourselves with our purpose once more.

> *If anything rings disharmonious, you must immediately examine its worth. This disharmony is a very clear signal to you that must not go*

> *unnoticed. And after recognizing the disharmony, it's from that that you discern what action to take. It's in your instinct. The more that you hear and attune your ear to the harmony, the clearer the music that comes through your life – the sweeter the melody. Trust the melody. If it's not pleasing to you, it is of little use to you. – Solomon*

We need to look at ourselves. Analyse our past: all that has happened, and why they have happened. Remember that every adversity is a lesson to be learned – and moved on from. Go as far back into your childhood as possible to recall what it is that you really loved doing, before you needed to forget what you came here for (as a result of conditioning) in order to search for that forgotten need once more. How would you serve those here on this plane? And how did you get to where you are now?

> *There is a chorus behind every endeavor in this plane. You are not alone in your work. There are multitudes of people or spirits who are bolstering every effort in your life. They appear as you become more conscious. They aren't necessarily going to stand and be photographed with you, but they are there to help your energy flow. At times you will feel them more clearly. And, also, because of your development, you are able to access them more clearly. They have always been there. You are suddenly seeing and feeling them. It's because your development has taken you to that stage. It will help you to understand that their efforts are your efforts. The entity of life is That Which Is, which is the great power that thrusts us all into various planes of existence. We are all a part of that great entity, that energy. – Solomon*

If you still feel stuck despite looking back at your past, and at all the lessons that you have experienced and learned from, you can do the following:

Lie on your back or find a comfortable position in a quiet place, just before you fall asleep. Take several deep breaths to calm your mind-chatter. Ask the universe to show or tell you what it is that you're here for. Give the universe a timeframe, if you wish. You can also mention for it to come to you in your dream, and you can ask to recall the dream clearly the next day so that you can record anything that came through. Relax. Listen out for anything that comes through. Notice any images that you see before you in your inner eye. Notice any feelings or smells that are "abnormal" to you. If you do not fall asleep by now, and if you're open-minded enough, you should be able to experience something coming through to you. If it doesn't happen the first time, do it over and over again over the next few nights. Something will flow to you. The important thing is to keep an open mind and notice anything and everything that comes through (which is not mind-chatter about your present situation).

It was through this exercise that I discovered something that I never even knew existed within myself. I had always said that I wanted to help people, though I didn't know how. Yet, I was frustrated with not getting anywhere in my life with regards to this soul-purpose of mine. Suddenly, from the conversations that I had been having with the universe, these internal conversations that I had with the energies mentioned by Solomon, it dawned on me that I had been suppressing a major fear all this while. I had a fear of people. I feared criticism. I feared that I was not enough; that I did not have all the knowledge and others would suppress me further when they found out that I don't know everything. My introverted adolescent world surfaced and I knew that if I were to grow, I have to allow others into my life just as others need to allow me into their lives. I have to break down the wall that I had put up to shield myself from others: my ego. I had to learn that there is power that comes from being vulnerable and to accept that there are lessons to be learned by opening up myself to others. As Solomon said:

> *Your work is such that it educates you as well as your clients and patients. It informs both. You should be growing as much as they are in the process. Don't deny the growth you will experience. It is your process. Your consciousness will expand in direct proportion to your ability to open your life to your client.*

I cannot expect others to open up to me if I am unable to open up myself to others whom I am here to help. That was when it clicked inside me. And it made me cry (in the dark, with the children fast asleep in the same room as me). I had come into this world as a "fearless" young child. I had come with leadership qualities in me. I was unafraid to voice my opinions if I felt that something was not correct or someone was being mistreated. I had the courage to stand up for that person. As a result of my confident self, I never came across school bullies as I had the power as a school prefect to tell off such bullies. I had a system to follow at school. I had respect from others around me because of my confident self.

In high school, I lost my own sense of self. At that age, the sense of identity, a sense of belonging as Earl Nightingale put it, was more important to me than cultivating my own sense of worth (of being an individual as well as being part of a collective in a constructive manner, not in the destructive manner that I was in). I was no longer who I was because I desperately wanted to *fit* in to the group. I could not afford to be individualistic as a teenager, a newcomer at school. I was forced to conform and my life spiraled downwards during those years in school.

I felt inadequate. As I read through "The Gene Keys" by Richard Rudd and looked through my halogenetic profile, my shadow of inadequacy truly resonated with me. I held on to the repressive nature of my profile, which incidentally also affected my physical, emotional and mental health. I was the one with "*consciousness… too afraid to look into the fear within its body, so it settles into the fixed patterns given to it by society.*" For those who are interested, Gene Keys was the brainchild of Richard Rudd, who believes that our DNA holds hidden meanings to our higher purpose, awaiting us to unlock the code so that we can bring in the essence of who we are into the world.

Looking back, my experience in high school was the experience I needed to have.

> *The function of being a means is not disjoined from the function of being an end. The sense of worth beyond itself is immediately enjoyed as an overpowering element in the individual self-attainment. It is in this way that the immediacy of sorrow and pain is transformed into an element of triumph. This is the notion of redemption through suffering which haunts the world. It is the generalization of its very minor exemplification as the aesthetic value of discords in art. – Alfred North Whitehead*

Without my bad experience, I would never have known or experienced the downside of being depressed. I would not have known how someone feels when they say that they feel that they are alone, with no one around who would help to support them. If I had not met the one person who turned my life around – the person who was supportive of me and stopped me from more self-inflicted pain and misery – I would not be able to help others feel the same way. In other words, in utilising the Law of Polarity, without experiencing the sorrow and pain, I would not have experienced the true meaning of triumph.

> *There is such suffering happening in the world, and our suffering leads us away if we allow it, but we often negate our suffering and somehow*

> become victim to it. *Suffering can bring immense joy – if it is focused. The lessons we exchange are those that continue from lifetime into lifetime.*
> *– Solomon*

Solomon's words rang true my heart: *Disregard that love affair with suffering.* It was through my bad experience that I savored and enjoyed by good experience. It was through my suffering in my adolescent years that I could experience the immense joy that life can bring: it is only a matter of our own choice.

> *Take inventory of yourself, see if any remnants of fear are standing in your way. Then you may grow... because nothing, absolutely nothing, can stand in your way. – Napoleon Hill*

I need to work on my fear: my fear of people and my fear of criticism by people. I need to be my childhood self again. I need to accept that there will be people who will criticise me and what I do. I just need to know that deep down in my heart, it is my soul-purpose in this lifetime to be of service to others, and I need to have the will and determination to get what I want. I need to persevere, as per my Gene Key suggests: *"If you are someone with 38th gift in your profile, every obstacle is a wonderful and vital opportunity to feel more alive and to fulfil your higher destiny."* Anything that stands in my way are only small obstacles that help me experience what I have set myself to experience; and to grow from. Obstacles are merely minor road blocks: we can learn from detours as well.

SEPARATION AND RECONNECTION

I am that, I am. - Exodus 3:14

Your purpose explains what you are doing with your life. Your vision explains how you are living your purpose. Your goals enable you to realize your vision. - Bob Proctor

Once we know what our life purpose is, as well as what our fears are, we work towards our vision of our purpose, conquering our fears and growing spiritually as we do so.

Set your mind on a definite goal and observe how quickly the world stands aside to let you pass. - Napoleon Hill

As Solomon persistently commented, "Don't think of the results; think of the process." It is the discovery and the action to realise our infallible vision which contains our soul purpose which helps us to grow spiritually.

It's the process of learning how to enjoy that's important – that you do not become a victim to an event, but derive joy from it, whatever the event may be. And what we do is train ourselves through our spiritual paths to view this suffering in an enlightened viewpoint to see how it will make us expand our growth within the universe. Then it becomes essential; it becomes fulfilling. For the whole experience. Do you reconnect and find the way to use that force in your environment to enlighten others around you, to increase the vibration of the quality of the experience? Your goal is to reconnect to it: separation, reconnection. Time: It's not linear; it's all happening at once, and we shift through various planes at the same moment. By removing your conscious judgment of what you're seeing, and allowing the infinity of that process to enter into your soul, you start to heal – you start to reconnect to that greater connection to that infinity of what you are. And you begin to access the answers that you need in this plane. Very simply at first, and then more specifically as time goes on. To find the moment where you're totally at ease – that's the beginning. Eventually it has to be that you allow it; you open the door for it. Open the door and let it come in (step 1). Step 2: helping others open their doors by being an example. – Solomon

So, what does Solomon mean in the discussion above regarding separation and reconnection? My theory is that when we are in the other realm, when we are at one with the universe, we are all interconnected. We feel everything. We know everything. We are one, yet we are many at the same time. We cannot separate our own individual feelings from that of the universe which we are made up of, that we are a part of.

When we come into this world, we are given the individuality that we desire when we are in the other realm. When we are in this physical world, we are given an ego (our individuality) and brought up in a world of separateness so that we may experience this separateness from the oneness. Anita described the separateness as something that we experience because we know what it feels like not to have that feeling:

"When we come into our bodies, we have consciousness and we have an ego," I continued. "That's why we call this a state of duality. But in the state of non-duality, we are pure consciousness – that is, there's only oneness. And in that state, we cannot know personal pleasure as a discrete experience because there is no pain separate from all other emotions or experiences. We cannot know joy as a separate emotion because there is no suffering experienced as a unique phenomenon. In the nonphysical realm, what we experience is unconditional love—the combination of all emotions and experiences of everyone and everything in existence. Unconditional love is what radiates from universal oneness. But here in this physical world, we are able to feel joy only because we know what it means not to feel it. We feel pain because we also know what it means to be without pain. We have contrasting reference points... In the state of non-duality, there are no reference points. There is no opposite. There is only oneness and unconditional love, which means there is nothing outside of self. Everything just is. It felt to me like we actually choose to come here so we can experience a reality of separation – and an ego is absolutely necessary to feel this reality and to experience these feelings. Without an ego, we would be back to the state of non-duality, the state of oneness, of pure consciousness." – Anita Moorjani, "What if This is Heaven?"

Moorjani also goes on to explain that we come into this world with two dials, turned to the maximum volume: one for awareness, one for ego. Over time, due to our social conditioning on this plane, our awareness dial diminishes, such that by the time we are at school, our ego dial seems to dominate more than our awareness dial, thereby, creating our sense of individuality. Recalling that we cannot experience what we are here to experience if we did not have our ego; having the ego dial turned on a higher volume than our awareness dial can be a good thing. However, in order to do what we need to do on this plane, we need to increase our awareness dial once again so that our ego and awareness dials are on similar levels.

Why do we need to increase our awareness? To carry out our life purpose, we need to reconnect to our oneness, to the infinite universe. "*I am that; I am*" references our separation as individuals on this plane, yet, our connection to the universe remains as we carry out our tasks, our life purpose. When we are at one with ourself (and the universe), we come from a place of infinite; a place of abundance where everything that we ever need or want to manifest into its physical realm is already made available to us. That is what true faith is: it is the knowingness that what we want is already en-route to us and we allow the universe to deliver it to us through the path of least resistance. That is what is meant by having faith and surrendering at the same time.

True manifestation comes from our need to love and serve ourselves as well as others; through our own expression of the universe. The physical conversion of the manifestation from an idea or a thought into its physical form comes at ease when we act from this point of being one with the universe, by serving the universe as well as ourselves at the same time.

Therefore, in all that we do, we need to come from our state of being: our state of oneness, of interconnectedness with the universe. In all that we do for ourselves and others, we need to be our true self - that which is connected to the infinite universe, because when we are in that "frame of mind", we come from a place of abundant love, creativity and gratitude and can thus transpose that abundance into the physical realm for all to realise and enjoy.

When we know what we want out of life, we can proceed with carrying out our purpose with an unwavering vision. We know that as long as we are operating from our true self, which is connected to the universe, for the benefit of all, we will be fully supported in our quest to become better ourselves and grow spiritually. As R Tagore said:

> *I slept and dreamt*
> *That life was joy;*
> *I awoke and saw*
> *That life was service;*
> *I acted and behold,*
> *Service was joy.*

In all that you do, rediscover you, be yourself and allow everything else to fall into its perfect place in your life.

SELF-DISCOVERY: THE POWER WITHIN YOU

Reconnect to the greater force that is. – Solomon

Do you know how much power you have within you? A Du Pont scientist once said that the atoms of your body contain a potential energy of more than eleven million kilowatt hour per pound. That is an impressive amount of potential energy that you have within you that you probably never even realised. If the electronic energy in the hydrogen atoms of your body could be utilised, you could supply all the electrical needs of a large, highly industrialised country for nearly a week! And that is just your physical body's potential energy!

It is unfortunate, however, that we take such power for granted. Earl Nightingale was right:

> *...things that are given to us for nothing, we place little value on. Things that we pay money for, we value. The paradox is that exactly the reverse is true. Everything that's really worthwhile in life came to us free – our minds, our souls, our bodies, our hopes, our dreams, our ambitions, our intelligence, our love of family and children and friends and country. All these priceless possessions are free. But the things that cost us money are actually very cheap and can be replaced at any time... But the things we got for nothing, we can never replace.*

If we pay attention to what we were born with, to what we already have, we would recognise the potential that we all have within us. Many philosophers and religions purport that we are – or at least, we are connected to – infinite. However, we tend to always look externally for confirmation of our ideas, of who we are, of our sense of "belonging." As Bob Proctor says, we have been brought up to "let the outside control what's going on the inside."Unfortunately, we live in a world where ninety-five percent of society are unsuccessful. In other words, we are looking for confirmation in the wrong place.

Throughout my high school years, I longed for a sense of belonging in a new environment. I was like a baby who had just been born: I allowed my subconscious mind to be re-programmed by my new environment so that I could fit in. Unfortunately, my subconscious mind was reprogrammed towards self-destruction. I learned that I was worthless, useless, stupid, and that I would never fit in anywhere. I became closed off. I thought that the world would be better off without a worthless crap like me. I began to feel alone and isolated from my environment, like a leaf drifting along the river, unable to control my life, and just going with the flow, towards a waterfall – towards my own destruction.

Solomon put it this way:

> *It's about recognizing your connection. Your connection to the infinite, to All that Is. And remembering that, recognizing that. All the answers are already there. All the lessons you need to learn you've probably already learned on some plane or another. They're all part of this package. Because if you are part of the infinite, you are also part of the infinite wisdom. You have access to that. You have all the answers you'll ever need.*

According to JJ Hurtak's, "The Keys of Enoch®":

> *Key 202-1: The Name of YHWH is coded within every biochemical function in our body, especially within the life-giving DNA-RNA matrix.*

Hurtak is implying that the universe/God/That Which Is exists within our cells. Scientists have indicated that our DNA as we know it does not form who we are. The rise of epigenetics in today's biological world is challenging that of the traditional DNA theory. As David Moore explained in his book "The Developing Genome":

> *Only 1.2% of the nucleotide bases found in the human genome are used in the production of proteins (or other products) that have some sort of a distinct biological function… more than 98% of this noncoding DNA is nonetheless transcribed into RNA at various points in development.*

> *It is now clear that the environments surrounding our cells are also able to control the genetic activity inside those cells… A second way noncoding DNA can contribute to gene regulation is by containing sequence infor-*

mation that can be transcribed to form RNA molecules that do specific things themselves, without ever needing to be translated into a protein.

The recognition that epigenetic processes influence the functioning of our genes means that our experiences and our DNA together makes us who we are, so our characteristics cannot be determined. The genome of an individual – that is the full complement of genetic material in that person's cell-is usually thought to remain unchanged across the person's life... genome of the human species is undergoing changes because of the process of evolution, but evolutionary changes occur in a population's genome across multiple generations, so these kind of changes are decidedly different from any changes that could occur in an individual's genome in a single lifetime.

In simple terms, our DNA does not fully control who we are, especially since ninety-eight percent of our DNA was initially considered as "junk DNA" by biologists in the early days. We are now finding that this nine-eight percent actually turns our DNA "on or off" depending on our internal and external environment. In other words, you only have yourself to blame!

I first came across epigenetics when I was researching about Dermatomyositis. The student doctors and registrars who interviewed us at the hospital always asked us if we had a predetermined genetic conditioning to it, or to other autoimmune disorders. Or if I had a difficult labour with him. We always answered that we had no family history and nor did I have a difficult labour with him.

Their queries got me curious. Was there really a faulty gene that I could blame? I became interested and I started reading everything that I could which I thought was relevant to the disease, including scholar articles online and the most recent cell research on autoimmune diseases. I never paid any attention to autoimmune diseases, nor did I even knew they existed, until my son was diagnosed with it but now, I made it my mission to find out all that I could to help him. I had a strong driver within me: *I am going to heal my son.*

Unfortunately, a lot of the information I found tended to blame something or someone else for the disease. The more I read, the worse I felt. It felt as if we're living in a completely toxic world which we cannot get out of, we cannot control, and we're all doomed to die with all sorts of complications from all the toxins that we ingest through our physical bodies. In fact, the first time I came across epigenetics was through YouTube videos purporting how our ancestors' diets and behavior affected us, generations down the line. It was the victim mentality that we are all so accustomed to.

I couldn't live with a victimised mentality. It was too painful. Something within me *knew* there was another explanation, but I just could not pinpoint the answer, until several years later when I learned and really understood that there is *always something good* in what appears to be an inherently bad situation. *We are never given a challenge that we cannot handle.* When I turned to look for the good in a seemingly bad situation, asking myself, "What can I learn from this?" things started to turn around 180 degrees.

Our body is made up of fifty trillion cells, with each cell having its own nucleus, DNA and function. These cells have two main roles in their lives: they listen and they respond to our behaviour, action and environment. How can this complex network of cells function as an organised whole? Dr. Gary Schwartz, a parapsychologist, author and professor and the Director of University of Arizona's Laboratory for Advances in Consciousness and Health proposes the following:

> *... here is a hypothesis that follows directly from the vision that the body is ultimately an organized energy system interconnected by a network of matrix of electromagnetic (and other) fields.*
>
> *Imagine that we had a huge symphony composed of numerous instruments and musicians. Each musician, with her or his particular instrument, plays a particular part in the score. How does such an orchestra ever play as an organized whole?*
>
> *If we were to look for a possible conductor inside the body, we'd seek out an organ that was centrally located, that generated a huge "downbeat" signal reaching every cell within the body, and whose signal conveyed essential information. The answer becomes obvious. The conducting organ would be the heart, not the brain. In fact, even if the brain happens to cease functioning – after an accident or some other trauma-the heart can potentially keep on beating and, with proper nutrition, the body can continue to survive.*
>
> *Think about this. The magnitude of the heart's QRS wave, when the ventricles contract, can be tens of thousands or hundreds of thousands of times larger than the size of an individual cell's electromagnetic field.*
>
> *Of course, no matter how good a given conductor is, the ultimate success of the orchestra depends upon the intentions and skills of each individual*

> musician. They must be willing and able to play together for the sake of the whole if the orchestra is to be successful.
>
> ... the body needs both a conducting heart, and a composing brain that provides a healthy score. The heart and brain must work together-not just physiologically, but energetically-if the body is to function as a whole.

Solomon continually refers to trusting one's heart throughout the book. In Greek, heart translates to the word, καρδία (kardia). According to Strong's Greek Dictionary, καρδία is rendered as the thoughts or feelings of the mind. Combining the Greek's definition of heart with Dr. Schwartz's suggestion that "There may be much more to our heart than its function as a mechanical pump," we start to see the correlation between our feelings and how we can affect the fifty trillion cells in our body. According to Gottlieb, an American psychobiologist, "... *people and things in the environment influence behaviour, behaviour influences neurons, and neurons influence genetic activity. Therefore, our traits emerge because of how various factors interact with one another.*" In other words, our cells are affected by our minds (thoughts and feelings), triggered by our actions and our environment (or by our own conscious thoughts and subconscious reprogramming, should we choose to follow that path), which in turn affect our (immediate) behaviour as the information is passed from the heart through vibration to a cellular level.

Looking at the stickperson diagram devised by Dr Thurman Fleet (a chiropractor, healer and teacher of metaphysics), the diagram which was introduced to Bob Proctor by Leland Val Van De Wall (Bob's mentor), we can see the truth portrayed by the simplistic diagram. The body really is controlled by the vibrational patterns of the subconscious mind, as Dr Lipton had discovered, prior to the discoveries about epigenetics. In addition to that, Dr Lipton also discovered how changing the culture medium of a group of cells, which come from the same parent cell, can turn into different body parts depending on the medium that the cells live in. The significance of this that *we are not victims of our genes*. We have the ability to change ourselves by reprogramming our subconscious mind and by following our heart. Our heart is the vibrational connection that we have to the infinite universe that has all the answers to our questions. It is that which is connected to everyone in the universe. The only problem is that we have been taught (and programmed) not to follow the heart.

When we follow our heart and do what feels right for us, we ignore the false rationalisations that come from our head. Besides, rationalisations are only limited to our experiences in this boundary filled physical world of ours. When we really allow ourselves to feel with our heart, and trust that feeling, as I had when I responded to my husband when he first asked me out, we realise that the heart really is our connection point to the universal mind.

Now, consider this: what if we chose the circumstances in which we come into this world, to learn the lessons that we wanted to prior to being "reborn", in order to experience the lessons that we have set for ourselves to the full extent of what we wanted to in order to grow our souls, whilst helping human kind through our actions and morphogenetic fields? Keep in mind also that we are connected to the universe through our cells, our external environment and our mind. "One Mind" by Larry Dossey gave numerous examples of how our individual mind is actually connected to a universal mind that is beyond our physical body. Anita Moorjani's "Dying to be Me" reiterated the same idea:

> *I felt nothing but unconditional love, both from her (Soni, Anita's best friend who had passed away years before her NDE) and for her. And then, just as I experienced that, it was as though my essence merged with Soni's and I became her.*

> *Although I was no longer using my five physical senses, I had unlimited perception, as if a new sense had become available, one that was more heightened than any of our usual faculties. I had 360-degree peripheral vision with total awareness of my surroundings. And as amazing as it all sounds, it still felt almost normal. Being in a body now felt confining.*

Solomon said that we are connected to the infinite. Moorjani described her near death experience (NDE) as this:

> *There I was, without my body or any of my physical traits, yet my pure essence continued to exist, and it was not a reduced element of my whole self. In fact, it felt far greater and more intense and expansive than my physical being – magnificent, in fact. I felt eternal, as if I'd always existed and always would without beginning or end. I was filled with the knowledge that I was simply magnificent!*

Imagine this: you are infinite. You can achieve whatever you truly want. The power within you cannot even be measured. An analogy was given as to how much power you can have in measurable (physical) terms, as highlighted by Nightingale yet most of us continue to live our lives complaining and merely going by our physical senses (as we have been so rooted in our conscious mind on this plane of existence). What if we were aware of our potential and use this infinite power to improve ourselves and those whom we draw into our lives?

Price Pritchett's book entitled "*you²*" shows us how we can achieve quantum leaps by negating incremental pathways to success. We can also now see that we have the infinite potential. If we were to combine this infinite potential within us with the infinite potential from our environment (i.e., outside of our physical being), we can achieve much more that our minds limit us to. As Pritchett puts it:

> *you² implies an "explosive jump" in your personal performance that puts you far beyond the next logical step. It's a formula for stunning advances in achievement and the realization of your dreams. The concept is one of exponential gains rather than incremental progress. You might compare it to multiplying instead of adding – it means a geometric progression in your effectiveness. That's exciting as well as provocative, but it gets even better. Remember, quantum leaps can come without apparent effort. These are high-velocity moves that carry you to dramatically higher performance levels without a time-consuming struggle. Quantum leaps seem to violate common sense… utterly! The idea of "moving to a higher orbit," and skipping several rungs on the achievement ladder in the process, strikes people as far-fetched, maybe even outrageous. After the fact, quantum leaps may be viewed as practical, sensible, even obvious moves, but they typically do not come to you as the obvious moves at the moment. Usually it's in retrospect that you perceive their hidden logic and elegance. Invariably, quantum leaps are not complex or intricate maneuvers. They tend to be simple, energy efficient, and time-saving.*

As Moorjani "reunited" with her father "in the other realm" during her NDE, she described what I felt was the true meaning of how our subconscious mind works:

> *I wasn't speaking those words, I was merely thinking them – in fact, it was more like I was feeling the emotions behind the words, as there was no other way of communicating in that realm other than through our emotions.*

Bob Proctor describes that our subconscious mind is our "feeling centre": it does not know reality from imagination. The subconscious mind acts on emotions. In "Napoleon Hill's Keys to Success: The 17 Principles of Personal Achievement", Hill likens the subconscious mind as the "film" in an old camera and the photographer as the conscious mind. The photographer has the ability to determine, sharpen, include and/or exclude images to be taken, and thus be imprinted onto the film. And, just as a photographer is always refining the composition and lighting of the image in the photo, we too have the ability to refine what we truly want in order to fully impress our ideas from our conscious mind to our subconscious mind.

Ancient Greeks referred to the subconscious mind as the heart; but what constitutes a spiritual existence? Solomon said:

> *I think we sent Einstein here to explain time. It's not linear; it's all happening at once, and we shift through various planes at the same moment. This thing called time – certainly, two-, three-, four-dimensional planes – is a yardstick of experience that is imposed upon the life-forms in terms of their ability to regenerate. But in actuality, that is extendable; that is, it's infinite… It's more multidimensional than that.*
>
> *By removing your conscious judgement of what you're seeing, and allowing the infinity of that process to enter into your soul, you start to heal – you start to reconnect to that greater connection, to that infinity of what you are. And you begin to access the answers that you need in this plane.*

Moorjani recounted her experience in a very similar manner to Solomon's description:

> *Time felt different in that realm, too, and I felt all moments at once. I was aware of everything that pertained to me – past, present, and future – simultaneously. I became conscious of what seemed to be simultaneous lives playing out. I seemed to have a younger brother in one incarnation, and I was protective of him (this younger brother is actually her older brother in this lifetime, and was on his way in a plane to Hong Kong to say his final goodbye to her in ICU).*
>
> *In other words, time didn't run linearly the way we experience it here. It's as though our earthly minds convert what happens around us into a sequence; but in actuality, when we're not expressing through our bodies, everything occurs simultaneously, whether past, present, or future.*

> *It seems as though our five senses limit us to focus only on one point in time at any given moment, and we string these together to create an illusion of linear reality. Our physicality also limits our perception of the space around us, confining us to only what our eyes and ears can see and hear or to what we can touch, smell, or taste. However, without the limitations of my body, I took in all points of time and space as they pertained to me, all at once.*
>
> *I realized that time doesn't move in a linear fashion unless we're using the filter of our physical bodies and minds. Once we're no longer limited by our earthly senses, every moment exists simultaneously.*
>
> *We think in terms of "time passing," but in my NDE, it felt as though time just is, and we're moving through it. This means that not only do all points of time exist simultaneously, but also that in the other realm, we can go faster, slower, or even backward and sideways.*
>
> *Because of this, I believe that when someone has a glimpse of what have previously been interpreted as "past lives," they're actually accessing parallel or simultaneous existences, because all time exists at once. And because we're all connected, it's possible to achieve states of consciousness where glimpses of others' reality seep through into our present moment, entering our consciousness as though they were memories.*

Both Solomon and Moorjani described us as multidimensional beings with infinite potential, in a timeless world. Metaphysical laws also support our multidimensional existence.

> *There are many planes of existence, Earth being one of the many. We all operate on various planes of existence, and sometimes simultaneously. It's multilayered. It's in all these planes as well that we visit past lives through the subconscious and bring up information that is integrated into this plane like a massive reference library, as it were. In your dream state you are consciously searching through the books. Taking one down, exploring, putting it back. But we forget most of it, because otherwise we wouldn't be able to function clearly in this life. Instinct is the imprint of those books in our lives. When you open that door, there's a vast amount of knowledge that is given to you, and at times, some of it is very specifically realized in this plane. – Solomon*

We are here on this plane to experience, to savor, to "be in the moment"; hence the time factor of birth and death. We would not be able to experience what we needed to experience, and go into the depths of our emotions if we did not feel the "time limitation" that is made available to us on this plane.

In some ways, I would have to say that my son's condition is a blessing in disguise. As difficult as it was for all of us, his condition made me reassess my priorities in life. Prior to him falling sick, I was a very methodical and materialised person: I had plans with regards to our savings, how we would invest our money and I never considered "lightening up" or going on holidays with the family. Back then, my idea of a holiday would be limited to visiting our closest relatives during Chinese New Year or to attend weddings, either in Malaysia or Singapore, going via the cheapest budget airlines that we could get a hold of. I would count every dollar that I spent, think thrice about buying anything that did not constitute as a necessity, and didn't really pay much attention to spending quality time with my |children. I was living for the future: I was always saying, "Next time" or "When the kids are older" whenever my husband brings up the idea of a holiday.

All that changed when my son fell sick, as in, very sick. When you're a parent who is faced with a situation where your child cannot turn in bed, cannot speak, is always clingy, always want to be carried, cannot pick himself up when he has fallen over on the couch, has ulcers all over his body, has blood in his stool, isn't eating and is choking on his on saliva whilst sitting up AND no one knows what it is or how they can help you, *you have no choice but to start having faith* that the universe is there to guide you. I was forced into that situation. I had no one who could tell me what he had, so I had to trust the ideas that came to me. I had to trust my feelings about the ideas that came to me. I had to act upon the ideas that came to me, the ideas that I felt I had to take action on. In essence, I had to stop living in the future and concentrate on living in the moment, believing that we would find the correct diagnosis for my son, so that he can have the right treatment for the diagnosis.

Mortality is a funny thing. We don't often think about it until we are faced with the situation, like I was. Perhaps that's why Abraham-Hicks once said that they love it when someone is faced with a terminal illness because it then forces them to do the only thing that the can do: to start living in the moment again, and to feel joy in living in the moment. That's exactly what I did. Though I didn't feel joy in living in the moment, I was expressing my gratitude for every precious moment that I had with my son. I was still breastfeeding him at the time, so I was grateful for every quiet moment that we had together. As Solomon said:

You need to understand the mortality.

Sometimes – well, often-it is essential that this perspective be there so that the experienced is fully realized. In other words, that you really take the time to smell the flowers, because time is limited. Well, in actuality, time is infinite.

But if you knew that coming in, there would be no attempt to really understand the plane you're in now, in terms of the value of the preciousness of the moment.

Part of what is special about the experience is the illusion that it has a beginning and an end. And that sort of gives it structure in terms of the experience of it. The quality of every moment that comes along, of the preciousness of that individual moment.

Now, once you start that process, add to it later the knowledge that it's infinite... infinite. If it's an infinity in terms of the whole structure of the life force, it even further enhances that rose that is being smelled.

To take full advantage of the plane you're in, you have to be rooted in it. And part of the rooting in this process is that beginning and middle and end. Once in the process, you reconnect to the greater force that is-All that Is-the rose in it becoming more enhanced because you've had the background. You've come through the trial of it and then have rediscovered your connection. It's a very beautiful process, ultimately. It's sort of like you bloom at the same time the rose does.

We live in a world where we are "programmed" by society, to cultivate ourselves and learn about the instrument that we are. As Solomon says, we are our own instruments but we play together in a symphony.

The real flow of energy will feel positive in your life. You will feel heightened by it. You will feel more alive. It's trial and error with you, because you're a specific instrument. You have to learn how to play yourself. No one has printed books on how to play you. Hear your own music.

We are here as individuals yet we are here to help one another reach our experiences in this so-called *life*. We are here to learn, experience and find ourselves, and in the meantime, we are here to help each other learn more about one another as we discover ourselves. Larry Dossey described it as a One Mind effect whereby the action of an individual can affect the greater "universal mind" that we are all tied to. Anita Moorjani said in her book:

> ...our biology responds to our awareness; our children, animals, and surroundings do, too. Our consciousness can change the conditions of the planet in a much larger way than we realize. This is because we're all connected – I can't say this often enough!
>
> In the tapestry of life, we're all connected. Each one of us is a gift to those around us, helping each other be who we are, weaving a perfect picture together. When I was in the NDE state, it all became so clear to me because I understood that to be me is to be love.

As Lynn McTaggart showed in her book, "The Intention Experiment":

> A great deal of evidence had already proved that all living tissue has an electric charge. Placing this charge in three-dimensional space caused an electromagnetic field that travelled at the speed of light. The mechanisms for the transmission of energy were clear, but what was unclear was the degree to which we sent out electromagnetic fields just by simple movement and whether our energy was picked up by other living things.
>
> Every movement we make appears to be felt by the people around us. Every intention towards someone else might have its own physical counterpart, which would be registered by its recipient as a physical effect.

We are all connected to one another, whether we realise it or not. We have the power to influence one another, whether intentional or otherwise. This connection is not affected by time or space, as shown by McTaggart and Moorjani.

I have personally had several encounters with this one mind connection. The one I recall most clearly was when I was suddenly awakened from my sleep at about 4am on one particular morning, sweat running down my spine. I recognised this feeling: it's the feeling that something bad has happened. I didn't know why I woke up (and though I cannot recall the dream that I had, I do not remember having a nightmare before I was woken up). My (then) boyfriend-now husband called me later that morning to tell me what happened (we didn't have mobile phones back then and still relied on land-lines so waking up the rest of the family at 4am was a "no go" zone). He told me he had a very close encounter early that morning, as he was returning home from his fishing trip. He was fatigued and didn't really recall what happened that morning apart from suddenly finding himself driving up a curb, and running over a road sign. He panicked, and thought he was going to die. He told me that at that very moment, he called out to me and saw me in his mind before he "woke up" and managed to drive off unharmed. When I asked him if it happened around 4am, he said, "Yes!"

Solomon has shown that we need to be rooted on this plane in order to fully experience what we have come here to experience. However, for us to continue on our spiritual growth, in the process of discovering who we are, our own power, ourselves as part of the infinite universe, we need to recognise our ability to learn to play our own instruments. We become who we are because of the process, not because we have reached a target that has been set. We need to learn the process of accessing the energy to and through us; not let our external factors and others' opinions control who we should be.

Earl Nightingale said:

> *Discover what course of life will fulfill your powers completely. What are your powers? Your unique abilities can provide great service to others. Discovering them is being true to yourself. That is integrity and reasonableness. Be truthful with yourself. Take the responsibility of making the best use of what you have. You have your mind, your talents, your time.*
>
> *Follow your strongest suit. Do what you can do and do it with all that is in you. Don't go with the flow – be true! There is an unfailing boomerang that will always come full circle back to you.*

In the words of Solomon:

> *Do not think of the target. Think of the process. Do not think of the bull's-eye. Think of the tension of the bow. Your heart will never lead you wrong. Leave the thought process behind. Don't send (energy). Receive.*

We need to tune ourselves in order to listen to and trust our intuition that is connected to the infinite universe. It is only through this tuning process, that we have the ability to access the universal information that is omnipotent, to bring forth the universal idea into its physical form on earth. As we connect to the universe through our intuition, we are also aligned with our true self, that which is a part of the universe. Failure to do so will only result in our failure to achieve what we have set out for ourselves in this lifetime.

SELF-WORTH

Self-worth is the understanding that you are the universe. – Solomon

Ninety-five percent of people do not succeed because of conformity. They tend to follow the herd, and unfortunately, they tend to follow the wrong herd. When asked, most people do not know why they are here or why they wake up every morning. People go to work because that's just what other people do. They let the external factors control their situation: they choose not to take control of their own lives. They blame other people for their circumstances because that was how they were brought up. They allow others to limit what they can and cannot achieve in their lives. When given the opportunity to take control of their own lives, most people choose not to; either because of their own self-limiting beliefs or because of their own paradigms.

Those who conform are those who cannot see themselves as being worthy of what they want in life. In other words, they have no or little self-worth. It is a sad fact that most of today's society is truly rooted in this belief. Their own behaviour makes them so. When people are told that they can re-program this belief and that they are worthy, most tend to disregard the idea, choosing instead to concentrate on the negative situations they currently see around them. The select few who choose to believe it are often criticised by their friends and family. Without a supportive environment, these people tend to return to their paradigms and self-limiting beliefs.

Solomon says:

> In terms of your own self-worth, you must know that you are worthy from within. The need for your fulfilment is often of a nature that requires attention from others. Your fulfilment is in yourself; you need to rely on yourself. In essence, you need to love yourself.

Self-worth is not dictated by the amount of possession you obtain, or what you can hold on to. Self-worth is about an inner being being fulfilled, and allowing that joy to surface through its life. You're in the wrong program in a way in terms of how you believe your self-worth will surface. You have bought other people's predetermined menus for success. Don't be disheartened. You must learn to redefine for you what is true happiness. And that will come from the search, and journey into your heart. All the rest is avoidance. You're looking for someone to heal you. Healing comes from yourself, from inside you. The answers are already there. No one can make it better for you.

Only you can heal yourself, from within. That is why our belief of self-worth is vital as part of our spiritual growth in this world. We need to start by loving ourselves for who we are, accepting our own strengths and weaknesses as they are right now. We start by disregarding the criticism that others have of us and looking within to discover our potential.

Moorjani described very clearly what she went through in her pre-NDE life:

The breakdown in my life came from my focus outward, the comparisons I made, and the competition this creates. I used to have the feeling that there wasn't enough for everyone, which causes greed and competitiveness. I needed to convince others to believe and think the way I did, instead of embracing our uniqueness and differences. All these feelings came from a view that the universe is lacking and limited, when it's actually infinite. It's capable of growing and encompassing as much as we are. It's up to us to expand and allow in as much as we want, but it has to be done from the inside out, not the other way around.

Previously, I used to pursue, feeling as though I had to do, get, and achieve. However, the very act of going after something stems from fear – we're afraid of not having what we truly want. It keeps us stuck in duality, because the focus is on the inherent separation between the hunter and the quarry. Now, however, I no longer chase anything. Instead, I allow.

The more effort I have to put into trying to attain it, the more I know that I am doing something wrong.

The process of allowing happens by first trusting, and then by always being true to who I am.

As can be seen in the previous chapters, I started analysing my journey thus far, from as far back as I can remember and up until this point in my life. I looked at my childhood, as that is where most of our "programming" begins. That is also where most of our beliefs originate from. I look for the good and the bad in my childhood and I discovered how I have changed as I grew up.

Your early childhood usually gives you a good indication what you have come here for. It is where you have come into this world as your true self, prior to being programmed by society. Go back as far as you can remember. Not as far as you choose to remember, but as far back as you can recall. That is because we tend to blend in more into our society as we grow older.

Our adolescent years can also have a profound impact on our growth. My teenage years were not the best. I conformed to my peer's expectations and experienced conflicts within me: my true self wanted to shine through, but my physical need to fit in was stronger than my calling. It was a difficult time for me, but now, as I look back on those years, it has helped me to understand that I had to go through what I went through in order to grow. Without my conformity to society's expectations, I would not have experienced the spiral of negativity that came with it; nor the liberation that I felt when I broke through that negative spell. It also allowed me to view it from someone else's perspective, to put myself in someone else's shoes.

Nightingale, Proctor and other motivational speakers all reinforce us that we are worthy individuals capable of getting what we want, as long as it is in harmony with nature's laws. Eric Pearl discussed at length the need for "rituals" by most energy healers at his seminar and what he said was very true: rituals were developed from a fear based principle, in thinking of ourselves as being not enough, such that we need other "accessories" to make us whole again.

Quoting Moorjani from "Dying to be Me":

> It's unfortunate that we keep searching outside ourselves for answers – in religion, medicine, scientific study, books, and other people. We think the truth is somewhere out there, still elusive. Yet by doing this, we're only getting more and more lost, appearing to move away from who we truly are. The entire universe is within us. My answers are inside of me, and yours lie within you, too. Everything that seemingly happens externally is

occurring in order to trigger something within us, to expand us and take us back to who we truly are.

Solomon put it this way:

Self-worth is the understanding that you are the universe. That you are in tune with other great life forces that are around us all. We are not isolated or incomplete. There's no need to make yourself whole. You are whole. It's the process of awakening to that in this life that is the business of energy in this field. To know that you are whole. You can call it self-worth, but you are great as you are in this plane. We have forgotten it, and we have been led to believe that we are not. Your self-worth is your opening the door to your perfection. That's why you're here - to remember it. It's like a treasure hunt.

So get in tune with yourself. Listen to your needs. Love yourself. Reach within to find the perfection that has always been there. As Solomon says, *"You are enough. Trust that."*

WE ARE INFINITE

In the tapestry of life, we're all connected. – Anita Moorjani

Most of us have been taught to celebrate our individualism, our uniqueness which makes us who we are. In essence, we are all individuals but we are all connected in what Moorjani refers to as the *tapestry of life*. Everyone whom we have encountered appear in our life to teach us something. We are all capable of influencing one another, as Dr. Schwartz puts it, there is, "*evidence (that) supports the notion that everyone... appear to have the ability to influence the energy state of animate and even inanimate systems. Once again, the implications for us all are profound.*"

> Although everything exists within this web of interconnection and we have access to it all, my world at any point in time is a tapestry made up of all my thoughts, feelings, experiences, relationships, emotions, and events up to that point. Nothing exists for me until it's brought into my tapestry. And I can increase or limit it by expanding my experiences and awareness or restricting them. I feel as though I have a certain amount of choice about what I allow into my observation. – Moorjani

> People understand if you care about them in a real way. They don't always understand cerebrally, but from their instinct they can tell the difference. Real communication is the life-to-life energy that we share. That's truth. That's what's real. - Solomon

Both Solomon and Moorjani (as well as other NDE experiences) showed us that time is not linear: it is how we perceive time to be on this plane. Anything that we do is a moment-in-time which affects the next moment-in-time but also the previous moment-in-time and the sideways moment-in-time. Everything is interconnected in a complex web of existence.

Greg Kuhn tried to explain how material comes to form in his book, "How Quantum Physicists Create New Beliefs":

> *The quantum field, by the way, is an unbound, unformed field of energy representing the possibility to become anything. It is an infinite ocean of energy that waits in a state of pure potential to be commanded to take concrete form– forming "things" and creating your material reality.*
>
> *You collapse the quantum possibility wave any time you awaken your senses and observe, which is an act that commands subatomic particles to abandon their state of potential and respond to your expectations in forming material objects. This process of creation is exactly why we can call this process a comingling of your innate energy with the quantum field from whence material objects emerge. Material objects are created solely in context with you.*
>
> *… it is your observations and, more precisely, your expectations that command the unformed field of energy to manifest into concrete, distinct material objects.*
>
> *Your expectations are derived unconsciously from your beliefs; what you believe will always dictate what you expect. Your expectations (which continually command the field of energy to manifest into physical reality) are created by what you believe.*

In other words, everything exists in a state of potentiality until the observer chooses to observe it, turning it from potentiality to reality.

As science (quantum physics) and spirituality slowly come together once again, we begin to see how the two are actually one. According to Kuhn:

> *Timeless awareness is where the observer, the observed, and the act of observation become one. During timeless awareness all possibilities are present, because you are actually in commune with the quantum field. This is why it is important for you (eventually) to hold beliefs of love/ joy/ appreciation in all areas, because true love/ joy/ appreciation is one of the best ways to experience timeless awareness. When you hold those beliefs, you lose the illusion of being separated from your object of love/joy/ appreciation. Think about times when you were spellbound by gratitude, love, or appreciation, such as seeing your child born or watching a spectacular sunset. You lose yourself in those moments; you become one with the "thing" you are observing and forget to think you are separate*

> *from it. When you no longer look at the object or skill you desire to manifest as an "object" to be attained, used, and from which to gratify and/ or satisfy yourself, you are in a place of love/ joy/ appreciation. You have entered the field of all possibilities. You are no longer something separate from that which you are observing, and your desires can be, literally, spontaneously manifest.*

Proctor always uses his stickperson diagram in all his seminars and courses. This is the image which shows two circles: a big one with a conscious and unconscious mind, and a smaller circle representing the body. Conscious mind is the mind that we have control of: it is the objective mind which consists of thoughts we hold and act on. I think of it as the pictures that we place into our minds, the frame and composition of the photo we wish to see. The subconscious mind is the subjective mind: it acts on emotions and has not the ability to reject as it doesn't think. Napoleon Hill likens it to the film in a camera. It accepts whatever the photographer chooses to frame it with. Thus, the images that we place into our mind (willingly or unwillingly) will in turn invoke emotions within us, which thus turn our images into reality through the principle described above by Kuhn. Our reality is what we have chosen to observe, whether that was done or subconsciously.

Kuhn demonstrated how the law of vibration actually works from a quantum physics point of view. This correlates with spiritual teachings that have been taught over hundreds and thousands of years.

> *"Ask, and it shall be given you; seek; and you shall find; knock and it shall be opened unto you. For every one that asketh receiveth; and he that seeketh findeth; and to him that knocketh it shall be opened."*
> *– Matthew 7:7-8*

UNIVERSAL LANGUAGE

We Are. – Dr. Wayne Dyer (through Karen Noe)

Throughout his life, Dr. Wayne Dyer taught the world the power of the words, "I am":

Anytime you start a sentence with I AM, you are creating what you are and what you want to be. – Dyer

Dr. Wayne Dyer was well known for his spiritual teachings with numerous books published on spirituality and self-help genres. One night, as I was going through my Facebook posts, I "accidentally" came across an interesting article on Wayne Dyer's afterlife. It was published in the "Elevated Existence" magazine (the first time I had ever come across such a thing), in which Dyer came through Karen Noe, a fellow Hay House author and medium:

"At one point, he (Dyer) said everyone was yelling at him after he passed, asking, 'Why did you leave?' and he said, 'Tell them I'm still here.'" … "He started talking to me about We consciousness and the unity of everyone and everything; the compassion for all of life; and that what a person does to oneself or another affects the whole," she (Noe) shares. "The most important thing he talked about is how we are all one, and we think because you are there and I'm here, that we are different people, but we are not."… Although one of the teachings he shared before passing was about the importance of "I Am" when it comes to creation and understanding God is within all of us, but now he realized it's really "We Are," Noe says. "He talked about how God is within each and every one of us with no exceptions, and we have to realize the divinity within all of us and the power that we have, because we have tremendous power, but we are unaware of it," she explains… One of the most important messages Dyer asked his family and Noe to communicate on his behalf was that he now has the ability to be present for whoever needs him at a moment's notice. He is only a thought away.

The article caught my eye because it reinforced what I have believed to be the important teaching from Moorjani through her NDE: it is that we are all interconnected and that in the "afterlife," we communicate through emotions. I have always felt that words and language were just means for us to get by with one another on this plane. If we were all able to communicate without words on this plane, there would be no need for interpretations of one's intentions through their choice of words. There would be no conflict because we would all understand each another perfectly.

Radin's "One Mind" and McTaggart's "The Intention Experiment" are just two of the many published books which show that we can communicate with one another without words. Hunches that we get about someone is an example of this universal language which most of us can relate to at some point in our lives. Telepathy is another example of how we can communicate with one another, disregarding time and space, without the use of words.

The same can be said for the communication within our own body. Several researchers such as Dr. Schwartz have found that the heart may be the point which controls the numerous integrative networks of cells in our body through the heartbeat (pulse). The vibration that is caused by the beating of the heart is able to send information throughout the body.

Personally, I feel that vibrations (emotions) are a form of the universal language, one that can be understood by all humanity even if we do not speak the same language. There are various ways of invoking such information within a person, such as through art, photography or music. Music conveys the emotions of the composer through sound. Art and photography convey the information through visual aspects which is then converted into emotions by the audience.

On a day-to-day level, at least for now, we may not be able to converse through our vibrations with another person whom we do not know very well. If it is with someone who is very close to us, we may be able to pick up their vibration, which is essentially, the emotions that they are feeling. My husband and I are on par in that sense: we usually know if the other person isn't quite their usual self. When that happens, we don't have to speak: we only need to hold the other person close to us until we feel that the tension or the problem has "melted away." And we just know when we need to be there for the other person.

There are exceptions to this, however. Bob Proctor is one of the few individuals who can pick up a person's energy and tell them exactly what they're like just by looking at them. Though he can pick up the other person's vibration, he cannot communicate it back to them without words because the other person is unaware of how they can communicate without words. That's why they are usually stunned by Bob's "magic trick." Psychics can also pick up a person's energy just by tuning into it. For the rest of us, it's something that we need to work on. When we are in tune with our emotions, with our own vibrations, we can begin to pick up on other people's vibrations as well. I find that the better I know myself, the easier it is for me to tune in to other people's emotions.

Would we be able to communicate without words in the future? I believe that we are heading in that direction. Yes, we are still using words, but we no longer need to physically speak up. The world is moving towards messaging and texting. Emojis are now being used more widely instead of words. And the moment we send the message, the other person, regardless of where they are in the world, receives it almost instantaneously, just like in the other realm. With the advancement in technology, the speed of information and travel nowadays, I sometimes wonder if we are actually here to recreate the other realm in the physical world.

Of the range of emotions that we feel, I believe that love is the universal language that is most easily felt by all. It is as if, in the core of our existence, we know that we are love. There is a saying: love conquers all. When we truly love someone, we let go of all the negative emotions that we experience. We trust them whole-heartedly. We forgive any wrong doing that they may have done. That is because, in order to truly love someone, you need to begin by loving yourself. You need to forgive yourself for what you believe needs to be forgiven. You need to trust yourself to do what you feel is right for you. You need to see yourself as the "I am" that is connected to infinity, the universe. You need to realise that you are, in essence, a perfect being. You are human on this plane to experience the syllabus that you have set up for yourself, before you come into this world.

To love someone else, you need to understand that we are all part of the infinite. We are all here to help each other grow and fully immerse ourselves in the syllabus that we have set for ourselves. We are a part of the universe, a part of God if you will. As the lyrics in the closing of Les Misérables goes:

> *Take my hand, I'll lead you to salvation*
> *Take my love, for love is everlasting*
> *And remember, the truth that once was spoken*
> *To love another person is to see the face of God*

PART 3

The Mechanics: How it Works

IT IS ALL VIBRATIONAL

Life caused you to create a vibrational reality. – Abraham-Hicks

Abraham-Hicks (where "Abraham" is a group consciousness from the non-physical dimension interpreted by Esther Hicks) has been purporting two approaches towards manifesting what we want in our lives: through the workshop, which is visualisation in our minds, and through meditation, which is more of a process of allowing it to happen. Abraham describes the process of manifestation and why most of us do not get what we want in the following quote:

> *Every subject is really two subjects: wanted and the absence of what is wanted. And you are in the vicinity of one or the other usually.*
>
> *When you want something, you are in vibrational alignment with what you want, then the more detail you give to it, more you think about it, the more good feeling thoughts you have about it, then the more you practice the vibration that allows it to flow into your experience. It's what expectancy is. Expectation is a powerful state of being because it means that what you want and what you believe are in the same place. So expectation is really a sort of defining of what your point of attraction is at any moment in time.*

He goes on the explain that if we want something which we doubt we will have, meditation, that is, the process of allowing, is a better tool for us to use, "Because in the absence of thought, your vibration will raise." Abraham goes on further to explain:

> *When you want something that you do not believe you have the means to... It feels like discouragement.*

You can't get there from discouragement but you can get there from joy... If it turns you on and lights you up when you think about it, then do all of that that you can but do it for the lighting up, not because you need the vehicle... If you're imagining and feeling good, that's success.

The last sentence is also impertinent in Solomon's message to us: "It's about the process."

If we already have faith that what we want is already there for us, then visualisation would be the tool to use. In other words, if we accept that there is already a vibrational reality of what we want somewhere out there, then, in the words of Abraham:

> *If so, then it's already in existence. The source is with you with it. It's the source calling you on the path of least resistance to the full realisation of it.*

Abraham explains that we have to be in a place of "uncondition" as he calls it:

> *Unconditional joy. Unconditional positive expectations. Unconditional. The vehicle isn't there but the joy about it is. Because when the joy about something is there, it has to morph into the full realisation of it. It is illogical. It cannot not be (for it not to). But you cannot be discouraged and go there... You gotta find the vibration first.*

So how do we know if what we are manifesting is turning into reality? Abraham said:

> *If something is giving you joy, then it's coming, but if you're afraid, it's not.*

> *When you get to happiness, all the manifestations that represent that have to flow into your experience, but if you need the manifestation to get to happy, then that's a conditional love that's backwards and that's what slows you down.*

As Moorjani pointed out, we are made of unconditional love. So, if we are here to express ourselves, as the unconditional love that we are, needing our manifestation to come true to make us happy disallows us from expressing our unconditional self. That is what Abraham meant by needing something to make us happy, and pointing it out as a backward move because, in order to make manifestations a reality, we need to come from a state of joy, from pure unconditional love, from the infinite source that we are; we cannot manifest good from a place of lack, as lack has its root in fear.

In some cases, manifestations do not occur. Abraham has an explanation for this:

> *On the one hand, you are spirit in physical bodies. On the other hand, you've come into this environment to manifest materially. That's why you're in this leading-edge environment. You're supposed to manifest into these wonderful material things, you see. We just want you to discover the unconditional alignment that feels so good. So, some are afraid that when they'll find that unconditional alignment and that the things won't matter and that they don't want the things to not matter because they want the things... And then you doubt instead of believe.*

We have been conditioned by our society not to want "things". That such wants for materiality is wrong because we have been taught that there is a limit to everything. That lesson has come from a place of fear; a place of lack and limitations. We have been conditioned to just accept things as they are and just to be happy. That is somewhat paradoxical for two reasons: yes, whilst we are here to express ourselves and we need to be happy with what we have, it does not mean that we have to accept everything as status quo. Status quo is equivalent to incapacitated growth and we cannot remain at that level. Abraham revealed that we humans have a misconception that Source (the universe, God, That Which Is, All That Is, whatever you want to call it) is perfect and stagnant, when in reality, Source is continually growing and expanding, and since we are a part of Source, we, too, need to keep up with Source through our continual growth and expansion.

We cannot grow if we do not push beyond our own limitations and beliefs. That is what has kept ninety-five percent of society where they are. They are too afraid of pushing their limits. They fear growth. They accept limits as the absolute truth, but never questioned what or where their limits come from.

Lack and limitations exist in the physical plane because of boundaries. When we understand that boundaries are merely a reality that is created by our beliefs due to our existence on this physical plane, and that it does not exist outside of our physical existence, we begin to open ourselves to a world of infinite possibilities and abundance. We are all a part of the infinite source, a part of the infinite mind. As we grasp the concept of infinity, we allow ourselves to tap into the abundant universe. When we *come* from a place of infinite supply, we no longer focus within the boundaries of our problems because we are able to look beyond our problems. Problems are not obstacles: there are lessons to be learned.

Abraham pointed out that many do not bring themselves to experience the *unconditional alignment* because they are afraid of finding out that the "truth" that they have been told are lies, and had this to say on the importance of manifestation:

> *It's right that you want things to manifest because manifested things are the leading edge, and that's what you are here about. And that's what we are here about helping you be about. And do not misunderstand. Do not think that the things that you are manifesting are only for you. They are the full manifestation of that which we desire also. So you are manifesters. You are the plucking of the fruit from the trees. You are the full fledge end result of all that we all exist about. Can you feel how important that is? So never feel uncomfortable about the material that is in the manifestation of things because this is the leading edge, and that's what we are all about. But find a way to be happy anyway before the manifestation has occurred. That really is the key. You gotta find a way to be happy in the un-condition.*

How do we learn how to manifest? There are plenty of books, recordings, audios, meditations that allow us to learn how to manifest. Abraham explains below how we can do that, but why most of us do not succeed in our manifestations:

> *…You can accomplish the uncondition of that small fortune. You could do it now. You could do it today. You could practise it everyday until that's the vibrational frequency that you have about that, and then, what happens is, that vibrational reality that is pulsing here and prese4nting itself to you in endless ways because you're now in the receptive mode and you get an idea… "Oh! I just got the best idea!"… And then you think about it and you kill it. You know when that idea comes, that's you. That's you being in your uncondition that is not opposing to what you want so you're in sync with what you want, the manifestation of it has begun. But if what you need is for that manifestation then what happens is you say, "Oh, it still hasn't happened" and then you return to the vibration that doesn't allow it to happen. And you do that… Over and over again. You get in the receptive mode, the idea comes and then you face reality. And that's what keeps you from allowing the momentum of that to gain speed.*

As Proctor said, we allow our reality to determine who we become. We've relied too much on our physical senses. We've been taught to shut down our creative mental faculties that connects us to the infinite universe. We need to practise on a constant basis, how to overcome our *uncondition*. By practising on a constant basis, we change our vibrations, and we learn to look at things from other perspectives, allowing for easier manifestation of what we want, because we have unconditioned ourselves from the uncondition vibration which we are in. As Abraham said,

> *"The universe does not hear your words. The universe hears your vibration. And you have to be in the vibrational frequency of what you want in order for it to move forward for you."*

MIND-BODY RELATIONSHIP

Your Body is Your Subconscious Mind – Dr Candace Pert

Bob Proctor adopts the "stickperson" diagram of having the mind controlling the body. It is a good way of introducing one to the mental picture of the relationship between the mind and the body.

Dr Candace Pert's findings, in some ways, do agree with the stick-person theory. She, too, believed that the brain is not in charge of the body. Over two decades of research, Pert revealed that biochemicals flow and resonate within the body, distributing information to all the cells (and their networks) simultaneously. In her description of how the cells operate in her book, "Molecules of Emotions":

> *If the cell is the engine that drives all life, then the receptors are the buttons on the control panel of that engine, and a specific peptide is the finger that pushes that button and gets things started.*
>
> *As investigations continue, it is becoming increasingly apparent that the role of peptides is not limited to eliciting simple and singular actions from individual cells and organs systems. Rather, peptides serve to weave the body's organs and systems into a single web that reacts to both internal and external environmental changes with complex, subtly orchestrated responses. Peptides are the sheet music containing the notes, phrases and rhythms that allow the orchestra – your body – to play as an integrated entity. And the music that results is the tone or feeling that you experience subjectively as your emotions.*

In essence, her findings show that the cells in our body can learn and affect what and how we feel:

> *Emotions are constantly regulating what we experience as "reality." The decision about what sensory information travels to your brain and what gets filtered out depends on what signals the receptors are receiving from the peptides. There is a plethora of elegant neurophysiological data suggesting that the nervous system is not capable of taking in everything, but can only scan the outer world for material that it is prepared to find by virtue of its wiring hookups, its own internal patterns, and its past experience. The superior colliculus in the midbrain, another nodal point of neuropeptide receptors, controls the muscles that direct the eyeball, and affects which images are permitted to fall on the retina and hence to be seen.*

This is why habits are so hard to break! Pert's research showed how our nervous system will only acknowledge what it accepts to be our normal, internal patterns, based on our past experience. It filters out the information that is required, and sends what it perceives as relevant instructions to the corresponding networks within our own bodily system so that we only see what we (or our cells) want (us) to see!

Our subconscious mind is on autopilot mode whenever possible. Hoobyar, Dotz and Sanders explained in their book, "NLP: The Essential Guide to Neuro-Linguistic Programming," that the mind has three favourite autopilot options:

> 1) Generalisation, which is noticing how an experience is similar to other experiences (and also contributing towards our limiting beliefs).
>
> 2) Deletion, which is dropping off aspects of an experience perceived to be uneventful.
>
> 3) Distortion, which is the change of an experience to a modified form of what it actually is.

In his book, "The Biology of Belief," Dr. Bruce Lipton showed how the conscious and unconscious mind work, separately and together:

> *The evolution of higher mammals… brought forth a new level of awareness called "self-consciousness," or, simply, the conscious mind. The newer conscious mind is an important evolutionary advance. The earlier, subconscious mind is our "autopilot"; the conscious mind is our manual control. The sub-conscious mind, the most powerful information processor known, specifically observes both the surrounding world and the body's internal awareness, reads the environmental cues, and immediate-*

ly engages previously acquired (learned) behaviors-all without the help, supervision, or even awareness of the conscious mind.

The two minds make a dynamic duo. Operating together, the conscious mind can use its resources to focus on some specific point, such as the party you are going to on Friday night. Simultaneously, your subconscious mind can be safely pushing the lawn mower around and successfully not cutting off your foot or running over the cat-even though you are not consciously paying attention to mowing the lawn.

The two minds also cooperate in acquiring very complex behaviors that can subsequently be unconsciously managed. Remember the first day you excitedly sat in the driver's seat of a car, preparing to learn how to drive? The number of things that had to be dealt with by the conscious mind was staggering. While keeping your eyes on the road, you had to also watch the rear and side view mirrors; pay attention to the speedometer and other gauges; use two feet for the three pedals of a standard shift vehicle; and try to be calm, cool, and collected as you drove past observing peers. It took what seemed to be a long time before all these behaviors were "programmed" into your mind.

Lipton's example of driving a car is a prime example of how we can intentionally use our conscious mind to reprogram our subconscious mind, to the point where we drive on autopilot mode once we are comfortable with our driving. Pert showed how this is done on a cellular level through the cell receptors within our body. In order to be able to "filter out" the required information, the cells would need to establish some form of memory, through either of the three autopilot options described by Hoobyar, Dotz and Sanders.

...the reason we can get stuck like this is because these feelings get retained in the memory – not just in the brain, but all the way down to the cellular level. This is how it works: As CRF levels increase in highly stressed infants and children, the receptors for CRF become desensitized, shrinking in size and decreasing in number. These changes happen when receptors are flooded with drug, whether it's drug your body produces naturally or a drug you buy at a pharmacy. The memory of the trauma is stored by these and other changes at the level of the neuropeptide receptor, some occurring deep in the interior of the cell at the very roots of the receptor. This is taking place bodywide. Although such changes can be reversed and need not be permanent, this takes time.

When we consider emotions as chemical ligands – that is to say, peptides – we can better understand the phenomenon known as dissociated states of learning, or state-dependent recall. Just as a drug facilitates recall of an earlier learning experience under the influence of that same drug for the rat, so the emotion-carrying peptide ligand facilitates memory in human beings. The emotion is the equivalent of the drug, both being ligands that bind to receptors in the body. What this translates into in everyday experience is that positive emotional experiences are much more likely to be recalled when we're in an upbeat mood, while negative emotional experiences are recalled more easily when we're already in a bad mood. Not only is memory affected by the mood we're in, but so is actual performance. We're more likely to be helpful to others and perform in altruistic ways when we are experiencing a good mood. Conversely, hurt the ones you love enough times, and they will learn to feel threatened in your presence and remember to act accordingly. It doesn't take an expert in emotional theory to recognize that there is a very close intertwining of emotions and memory. For most of us, our earliest and oldest memory is an extremely emotion-laden one.

Pert showed how our emotions relate to our actions, and why we feel the certain emotions pertaining to particular activities that we do. She went on to say that "emotional states or moods are produced by the various neuropeptide ligands, and what we experience as an emotion or a feeling is also a mechanism for activating a particular neuronal circuit – simultaneously throughout the brain and body – which generates a behavior involving the whole creature, with all the necessary physiological changes that behavior would require. – Candace Pert

Pert's findings correspond with a quote by Earl Nightingale: *We become what we think about.* Whilst Proctor continually reminds us that most of us are too reliant on our external senses, creating our own (unwanted) reality, it appears that on a cellular level, the receptors are also doing the same thing for our body subconsciously. Perhaps that is how we end up where we are.

Therefore, in order to change, mere conscious thinking of what we want will not help us to achieve our dreams or desires. We need to reprogram our habits, our paradigms as Bob Proctor calls them, so that our cells will in turn reprogram our mind and body to concentrate on looking out for the reality we wish to create for ourselves. The internal network reprogramming will change our emotional state, thus forcing us to "kick ourselves into action" to go for our dreams. From a quantum physics point of view, everything is omnipotent and remains in its potential state until it is realised and turned into reality by the observer. To quote Dr. Lawrence Walter Ng:

> *In order for things to change, I must change first.*

An important thing to note though from Pert's findings is that these memories, which affect our emotions and thus, our actions, are embedded deep within the cellular level. In order for these memories to fully embrace the new experience, they need to go through a process of "deletion", as mentioned by Hoobyar et. al. Our body cannot feel two opposing emotions at the same time: one or the other needs to dominate. As Pert mentioned in an interview in her audiobook, "Your Body is Your Subconscious Mind," "*you cannot tell your foot to be angry and your hand to be loving at the same time.*"

Anita Moorjani revealed in her book, "Dying to be Me":

> *It's about allowing what I'm actually feeling, rather than fighting against it. The very act of permitting without judgment is an act of self-love. This act of kindness toward myself goes much further in creating a joyful life than falsely pretending to feel optimistic.*
>
> *It's about trusting the process even as I face a difficult time and not being afraid to feel anxiety, sadness, or fear, rather than suppressing everything until those emotions pass. It's about allowing myself to be true to who I am. Because of this, the feelings will dissipate and occur less and less frequently.*

Moorjani explained that the most effective way to delete unwanted memories from our mind (and thus, our cells) is to completely embrace our emotions, from a loving perspective, and letting the feelings pass. She said that the true act of self-love is to allow one to fully feel the emotion-without judgement.

Anytime we feel strong emotions within us, we need to take the time to feel it within us. Suppression of negative emotions in particular can lead to further disharmonies between our mind and our body, bearing in mind that our fifty trillion cells that make up our body have memories as well. Suppressing our negative emotions will trigger changes deep within the interiors of our cells, at the roots of the receptor as they become desensitised to such emotions.

The universal language – the language of "the other realm – is that of emotions. Vibration or emotion is the only way we can communicate with the infinite mind, the universe. We cannot feel different emotions all at once in this physical realm: we may be able to feel different emotions in short bursts, but we cannot be happy and angry instantaneously for example. Remembering that we are here to fully experience the depths of emotions, it would not serve us to suppress any negative emotion that we may be experiencing. Take the analogy of a grass root as the roots of our cell receptors. If we throw some sand onto the grass, it is logical that we cannot see the sand as they are hidden between the blades of the grass. However, if we dump a heap of sand onto the same patch of grass, we can no longer see the grass. Do this for your entire lawn, and soon enough, there will be no patch of grass left – only sand can be seen. Similarly, "physically changing" the environment that the cell receptors exist in will make the receptors become desensitised to the environment. If we desensitised the cells sufficiently, it will produce a completely new environment for the receptors to learn from and react to. The desensitisation may lead to issues in other parts of our body or our minds, depending on the clarity of the network of communication between the cells in our body.

That is why it is very important for us to fully allow – without judgement – the feelings or emotions that we feel. Some people refer to intuition (from the universe) as a "gut feeling". That is how we maintain our communication with the infinite. In such situations, we also allow ourselves to just "feel". It is when we apply our conscious mind, our "logical" reasoning, that we tend to ignore these gut feelings that we experience. Most of the time, this ignorance is when we allow our conscious judgement to come into play, and we "fog up" the intuition that is coming to us.

Hoobyar, Dotz and Sanders demonstrated how memory actually works in their NLP book:

> ...*you store a highly customised version of your past, what may have actually happened and WHAT YOU THOUGHT ABOUT IT AT THE TIME. Every time you revisit a memory, you see what really stood out for you... In other words, the foreground of the memory gets sharper with repeated visits. The "background" gets duller and dimmer each time you remember the important part and ignore the rest, which changes the memory even further. This means that there are NO accurate and*

> *complete memories in a human mind. Basically, your own personal history is a moving target. It shifts each time you call up a memory.*

In other words, it is possible to change your memory by shifting your focus using your conscious mind. Once we have fully experienced our negative emotions (and it has to be fully experienced, given the sand on grass analogy explained previously), we can tactfully use our conscious mind to look at the event from another perspective. Such is the power of perception. One's ability to change the perception of a situation is dependent on how often he or she chooses to look at that situation. By changing our perception, we retrain our mind and therefore our cells, to look at the situation from another point of view. The cells will then send the signals to the brain to increase its awareness from that perspective, and we then see and feel it in the physical world from the alternate point of view. The more we practice doing this, the easier it is for the cells to recognise and send such signals to the brain to "watch out for" what we consciously set ourselves to "watch out for."

Everything exists in a state of potentiality until it is observed and turned into reality by the observer.

FROM THOUGHT TO FORM

No thought of form can be impressed upon original substance without causing the creation of the form. – Wallace D Wattles

Man is a thinking centre, and can originate thought. All the forms that man fashions with his hands must first exist in his thought; he cannot shape a thing until he has thought of that thing. – Wattles

James Allen (a British philosopher) and Earl Nightingale compared the mind to a garden. The seed in which we plant in our own garden (of mind) are the thoughts we choose to hold and internalise. The soil does not care what you plant in it: we may choose to plant apple seeds that will grow to produce apples for us and those around us or we can choose to plant seeds that turn into a poison ivy. The choice is ours, but we first need to be aware of the type of seeds which we plant.

On water turning into ice: so in our lives, we metamorphose in various forms. And each form can be looked upon as a creation. But in actuality it is an energy transfer. – Solomon

We have been given the gift of mental capacity to think for ourselves. It is up to us to plant the seeds in our own garden. What do you choose? Seeds that harm you and others around you? Or seeds that sustain your growth and benefit human kind? We are here to experience, grow and help one another in this immaculate and complex tapestry of life. Harming ourselves through negative choices will not only affect ourselves, but also those closest to us. The opposite is true for if we take care of ourselves, and continue to advance in life, we become role models for others to follow suite. Not only do we then have an abundance of all that we want in life, we also inspire others to work toward their soul advancement, thus, raising our interconnected lives to a higher vibration.

Your life is created, and it is reflected in the environment. It's not the other way around. You create the circumstance in which you find yourself as well. – Solomon

Quoting Genevieve Behrend from her book, "Your Invisible Power":

This same power that brought universal substance into existence will bring your individual thought or mental picture into physical form. There is no difference in the power. The only difference is a difference of degree. The power and the substance themselves are the same. Only in working out your mental picture, it has transferred its creative energy from the Universal to the particular, and is working in the same unfailing manner from its specific center, your mind.

Your mental picture is the force of attraction which evolves and combines the Originating Substance into specific shape. Your picture is the combining and evolving power house, in a generative sense, so to say, through which the Originating Creative Spirit expresses itself. Its creative action is limitless, without beginning and without end, and always progressive and orderly. "It proceeds stage by stage, each stage being a necessary preparation for the one to follow."

We are energy. We are interconnected to one another. Numerous studies have shown this to be true, such as those by McTaggart, Radin and Schwartz. Dr. Bruce Lipton, author of "The Biology of Belief" goes a step further suggesting that not only are we connected to each other, we are also connected to microorganisms through our cell structure: that the fifty trillion cells that make up our body have the memory of millions of years of evolution from the single cell organisms.

Dr. Masaru Emoto, a Japanese author and researcher, showed how we can affect the formations of water crystals simply by applying our thoughts and intentions. Since then, others have tried similar experiments on plants and cooked rice with the same results. Negative thoughts or contaminated water resulted in deformed or even unformed crystals. Positive thoughts resulted in beautifully created crystals. What was even more interesting was his finding that the water sample which he took from Tokyo just prior to a major earthquake in Japan refused to produce any crystals. It was as if the water "knew" there was inherent danger coming.

We do not have concrete scientific evidence which support how thoughts can affect crystal formations. However, one thing that I do know is that everything is vibrational. Words, whether they're written or spoken are vibrational in nature because the intent of the words are vibrational. Thoughts are also vibrational. Since *everything* in the universe is interconnected, it means that our vibration is transferred from us, through the universe, to the other person or object. This explains why the water crystals form beautiful crystals when it is "bathed" in positive intentions, whilst the ones exposed to negative environments result in deformed crystals. As to how the water in Tokyo "knew" there was going to be an earthquake, it would be suffice to say that when you are fully connected to the universe that knows *everything*, in an environment where you are not bound by time or space, you would be prepared for what is coming and nothing comes as a surprise for you. This goes back to Solomon's analogy of time: if we were not given a time limit and we came here knowing that life is infinite, we would not stop to fully appreciate the roses around us.

Based on the *one mind* theory, if we are made of the same energetic material as other seemingly inanimate objects such as rock and water, this is evident that not only are we connected to one another in the *universal mind*, we are also connected to nature in the same manner. Consequently, listening to our intuition is in simple terms, our ability to connect to the universal mind. Proctor said, "Prayer is when we're talking to God. Intuition is when God is talking to us." He continued on to say that most people call out to God for help, but then leave the receiver hanging off the hook so we cannot receive the message that comes through.

> *Trust is the removal of doubt - the absence of doubt - that the message is undeniably clear and true ... A message can only be understood when it's fully trusted. – Solomon*

Animals trust their instinct: that is why we find them on high grounds when they sense a major flood is coming. That is why we do not see butterflies just before it rains. However, we as human use our rational minds so often, that we've ignored our instincts which are connected to the universal mind (the infinite, the universe). We've learnt only to trust what we can sense through our physical senses as that is how we have been brought up.

> *It is not a cerebral exercise for you. I can underline this. For you it is necessary to touch a greater part of you that has remained hidden. That's the lesson for you. Should you undertake it, you will achieve greatness. You are working at it. You need to let it work you. Your interference and*

speculation are counter-productive to the energy flow. You get in its way, and you stop it. You mustn't allow yourself to constantly question your power. You're in its way. Get out of the way. Let it flow through you without question. Acknowledge the force within you, and let it play you, as an instrument. Don't constantly question the tightness of the strings; let the music happen. You are in a manipulative manner when you try to gauge it. To get it. To reach for it. It's already there inside you. Your frustration of trying to open and get out of the way become a clear vessel is part of the problem. – Solomon

What are our instincts? How do we learn to trust them? Solomon said:

Our instinct is the sum total of All That Is. We clear a path. That is instinct… that is what guides us. Trusting the instinct and discovering it.

I want to emphasize the connections we all have. Reinforce them. Without them we have lost.

There is a collective mission here. That mission, in essence, is reaching out in any way you can. It's so important. That contact, that interaction, is where information is exchanged, more than on a verbal plane. It is energy being exchanged.

If the quality of energy is of a high plane, it gets exchanged. And it blossoms in another individual. And it's not what's being said. It's the intent. So by reaching out from a higher perspective, we are creating a higher energy among us all. And that higher energy comes from instinct – our instinct. And learing the path to it cannot be underestimated, though there is a problem sometimes of "Are our ears listening to 'instinct,' or are they listening to 'negative voices'?" The quest for instinct will define it for you.

We are about accessing information, all of us. We access it. Process it. And exchange it. It goes out into the world like a pebble thrown into the water, creating ripples of effect. That is what you do by creating value.

Most of us have been brought up in a society where we trust others' opinions more than we trust ourselves. Or, at the very least, we need confirmation and acceptance from others for the decisions that we make. In doing so, we disregard the instinct within us. The act of listening to our own instincts, which essentially is guidance from the universe (as we are all part of the universe), is like training a muscle in one's body: the more you use it, the firmer the muscle.

> *Trust your heart; the answers are there. It's about guidance. That is what the process is about, your own life discovery. If anything rings disharmonious, you must immediately examine its worth. This disharmony is a very clear signal to you that must not go unnoticed... The more that you hear and attune your ear to the harmony, the clearer the music that comes through your life - the sweeter the melody. Trust the melody. If it's not pleasing to you, it is of little use to you. – Solomon*

We need to trust our instincts; the ideas and feelings that come to us as hunches. We need to have faith that our ideas which essentially come from the universe, can be converted from thought into reality, through the use of our mind and body as the instrument of conversion. The subconscious mind helps us to "listen," the conscious mind allows us to think and accept whatever ideas we choose to accept, whilst our body does the actual work of converting from an idea to reality. Quoting Robert Sharma:

> *Everything has been created twice, first in the mind and then in reality.*

One's faith is very important during this process. It is the superglue which holds together two vastly different objects. The strength of one's superglue at the end of the bonding process can be likened to one's will to hold onto the faith that their idea will eventually materialise. If, at any time, one loses grip between the two objects held together by the superglue during the bonding process, the superglue will be rendered useless. Similarly, if one quits just before the idea is turned into its physical form, one will render the idea, or worse still, themselves, as being useless. Quoting Napoleon Hill:

> *FAITH is the head chemist of the mind. When FAITH is blended with the vibration of thought, the subconscious mind instantly picks up the vibration, translates it into its spiritual equivalent, and transmits it to Infinite Intelligence, as in the case of prayer.*

When we ask a question, and tune into our intuition (without judgement), the answer, which is omnipresent, will come through to us. When we combine that thought with our determination and faith that it will get us to where we are heading towards, it is turned into reality by our desire and sheer will to act on our thought. The key is to *listen*, and *act*.

> *You can be anything you want to be, if only you believe with sufficient conviction and act in accordance with your faith; for whatever the mind can conceive and believe, it can achieve. – Hill*

How does someone achieve his or her goals? How does it turn from an idea into form? Napoleon Hill's book, "Think and Grow Rich" provides the philosophy of being successful. The main idea of the book is that when you do what you love, you will have the will, faith and determination that your desires will come true.

Loewenstein explained in his book, "Physics in Mind: A Quantum View of the Brain," that Einstein's theory of relativity is a space-time co-ordinate. He also explained that *"the times for reversals to happen in the molecular world – or "Poincaré's recurrence," as it is called – go up exponentially with the number of molecules in a system: 10^N seconds for a system of N molecules. Which even for a simple system like a drop of saltwater, comes to $10^{10,000,000,000,000,000,000}$ seconds or $10^{1,000,000,000,000}$ years."* In essence, there is a very remote chance that time can move backwards in the physical world. *Nothing is impossible.*

Remember, that in a non-physical world, time is essentially limitless and non-linear, as explained by Solomon (through Einstein) and Moorjani. Thus, setting a goal in the space-time co-ordinate in the "future" is similar to setting a point in a co-ordinate system. Mary Morrissey, a coach, speaker and spiritual author, made a very interesting point in "Magic in your Mind":

> *You do not get to your dreams. It's literally impossible to get to your dreams. You've got to come from your desires.*

What Morrissey is saying is that in coming from our desires, we are connected to the infinite universe, to the non-physical world. To come from our desires means that we have already received the answer to our question from the infinite universe. The very thought that comes to us means that it already exists somewhere in the universe, as a co-ordinate.

I believe that faith is like the arrow on a vector: it helps one to get to that co-ordinate. I see will and determination as the speed of the vector: the stronger one's will and determination to get what he or she wants, the faster the vector travels. According to the law of vibration, which is the primary law of the universe, the stronger our will and determination to get to our goals, the easier and quicker it is for us to move in harmony with the universe to get there (the co-ordinate or possibility has already been set in the infinite universe).

We may have set a point in the co-ordinate system to get to, but we may not be able to see how we would get there. In our physical world, with its boundaries and limitations, we are not privy to see *all* the potential ways for us to get to our goals because we have been conditioned (programmed subconsciously over the years) whilst we are rooted on the physical plane. This is where the universe steps in and guides us in the right direction. If, as we work towards our goal, things continue to happen to keep holding us back, we need to stop and look at what is going wrong from an "aerial" point of view. This is where Pritchett's story of the fly hitting against the glass window comes in. There was a fly, determined that there was only one way of getting out to the open, and that is through breaking the glass window: it refused to stop, take a step back and turn around to notice the open door behind it. Because of its inability to "listen" to its intuition, its guidance from the universe, the fly dies there on the window sill. Sometimes, if things do not go as planned, it may be the universe trying to tell us that there is a better way to get to our goal.

> *If anything rings disharmonious, you must immediately examine its worth. This disharmony is a very clear signal to you that must not go unnoticed. – Solomon*

It is possible to get what you want, but only if you take action and have the willpower and faith that you will get what you want. Pam Grout's "E^2" and "E^3" books contain numerous small-scale experiments that you can try out for yourself, as I have succeeded in doing. Once you have built up your confidence, you can then use it on your goals and aspirations in life. Always keep in the back of your mind, the story of the poignant fly in Pritchett's "you^2" book. It helps to keep your goal in check from an aerial or a bird's-eye view to make sure you're heading in the right direction.

F.E.A.R

Fear is only the absence of love, just as darkness is the absence of light. – Eric Pearl

Fear. It is something that we all have. It is something that has been instilled into us ever since we were young. We carry it with us wherever we go. Yet, have we ever asked ourselves where this fear actually stems from? Why do we carry it around with us constantly?

Pearl explained it in his book, "The Reconnection: Heal Others, Heal Yourself":

Fear is only the absence of love, just as darkness is the absence of light. Just like when you shine a light into darkness and the light becomes the only thing present, when you bring love into a place where there had been fear, you find that fear is there no more.

In other words, we fear what we do not know. We fear the unknown. What is an unknown? I define an unknown as something that we have yet to explore because we have been living, acting and behaving within the confines of our own limits. Who sets our limits? Who sets our perceptions? Who sets our paradigms? Who sets our behaviour? Why do we fear to go beyond our limits? What is it in "comfortability" that stops us from looking beyond our perception of our own life?

The truth is, we have been conditioned like this, ever since we were born. Research has shown that a child's mind remains in its hypnotic, subconscious state up until the age of seven. When we were still young, innocent, when our mind was constantly absorbing everything that we experience – see, feel, taste, touch, smell – we took everything in as being the truth. We were told what to do. We were told how to do it. We were shown the way. We were allowed to explore – but only within the limits that our parents and guardians set for us. As we become adults, we carry forth all such beliefs as the truth. Why? Because that was what we were told as being the truth. Now there is no one else to tell us what to do, or where to go, or how to live the life that we truly want. We have no guidance. The only guide (or boundaries) that we have been taught are our paradigms which have been programmed into us from a very young age.

What is it that you really want? When we were little, we were told how we should live our lives. Our parents would say, "You are going on to university after you finish your high school." We were given a direction and taken by the lead. Great. So what do we do after we "finish our education"? Society tells us "to work, be comfortable, have enough savings for retirement and then we die". In Proctor's words:

> *Most people tiptoe through life hoping to make it safely to death.*

Is that what we *really* want in life?

Our paradigms. Our beliefs. Our habits. We can blame it on our parents. We can blame it on our upbringing. We can blame it on society. We can blame it on our health. We can blame it on our bad luck. No matter how you choose to look at it, there is always someone or something to blame other than ourselves. What is the definition of blame? Merriam-Webster's online dictionary defines blame as *"to say or think that a person or thing is responsible for something bad that has happened."* The key word here is responsible.

I refer to *blame* as **Being Latent And Making Excuses.**

I choose to look at our social conditioning, our paradigms from a different perspective. Instead of asking myself the question, "Why (is everything that is bad happening to) me?" I ask myself, "Why did I choose to be exposed to all that I have gone through, from my childhood up until this point in my life? What can I learn from everything that I have experienced so far?"

I believe in soul contracts. I believe in reincarnation. I believe it when Solomon said that we chose our own syllabus before we were born. I believe that we have come here to experience our own syllabus, so that we may learn from our past experiences. For instance, if we have chosen to come from a poor family, it is because we have chosen to experience poverty at the deepest level within ourselves so that we may break free from it later on in life and teach others who are poor that they too can change their lives, just as we have. That is a "breakthrough" possibility. Or, we may have chosen to really live life with lack and limitation to really experience the opposite spectrum of abundance, which is where we all come from.

If we have come into this lifetime with a disability, it may be to teach ourselves that we can push beyond our limits, and also show others around us that we are capable, creative beings who can make our lives worthwhile despite others' judgement of our abilities.

There are lessons in everything but are we ever in the moment where we stop to think about what is actually happening to us? And why?

When we live in fear, we hand over the responsibility of our own lives to events, situations, or other people. Zig Ziglar, author and speaker, said that fear is *False Evidence Appearing Real*, because we take the "evidence" as being the truth and turn it into reality through our free-will, on our own accord. Yes, we have free-will. Whether we recognise this free-will or not is dependent upon our perception. We see what we choose to see: therein lies our free-will.

> *When I was in the other realm, where the layers upon layers of my values and beliefs were stripped away and I was left facing the truth of who I am at my core, I learned that two primary forces – love and fear – had been driving all my behaviors. One or the other of these two forces was behind every single action I ever took, and I could clearly see that I'd in fact spent most of my life being driven by fear, not love. I understood with a sudden stunning clarity that to transform my life, whatever I said or did from that point on would need to come from a place of love instead of fear. – Anita Moorjani, "What if This is Heaven?"*

As Moorjani said, our behaviour either stems from love or fear. So, imagine what our world would be like if we dispel the blame we have for everyone, everything and every situation that we encounter.

What if we removed this blaming business that we are so familiar with, this fear within us, and start taking charge of our own life? After all, we have come into this world through our own syllabus – our own creation, our own free-will, our own accord. Surely we owe it to ourselves to live the life that we really want in this lifetime. In other words, instead of blaming, we take *responsibility for* our own lives. Now, fear takes on a new meaning: *Face Everything, Accept Responsibility*.

When we choose to live in this manner, we will see that Pearl is correct: fear is the absence of love, just as darkness is the absence of light. When we are no longer afraid of the unknown, of the dark, of what lies beyond our limitations, when we begin to explore beyond our limits of ourselves, we will find the true expression of love that we are. And when that love, that light, shines all around us, we can then see the immense creative power within us to create the life that we really want and deserve.

It all starts with removing blame and fear from your life, and taking responsibility to lead and create the life that you *really* want.

PROCESS IS PROGRESS

The important thing is that you move. - Solomon

Process is progress. Process is what gives one the satisfaction in achieving one's aim or goal in life. Quoting Solomon: *Eventually there comes the point where these experiences mount in the spirit to recognize*: There is a bigger picture that I want to see all at once. There is a need for me to understand why this, this and this. And I can't do it anymore through a very narrow perspective, through this technique. I've experienced it through the perspective. But now I need to experience it as a whole, to see it without being restricted to that specific area of my life. *So we search to be able to see the grand picture. And, in doing so, we have to put the telescope down and trust that we will see it with our souls.*

> *The purpose of being given that limited telescopic type of view is to overcome it. It's the ability to want the wisdom, to see the big picture. It's like a high jumper who needs to go over the top bar. The bar is there so that the person can jump over it. It becomes the obstacle, and jumping over it becomes the reward. We're given an ego. The reward comes when we're able to let it go and see the bigger picture. We're not born seeing the bigger picture, because there is no experiential knowledge gained from that. It's the experiential path that we need to tread to see the big picture. If everyone was given the big picture immediately, no one would appreciate it, nor would anyone understand the process it took to see the big picture. There is nothing gained in automatic comfort, nor can it be appreciated.*

Reconnective Healing practitioners tend to see the above as a need to "disintegrate" a technique in healing. I feel that it can be seen from a wider perspective: it can also be a description about life itself. Earl Nightingale said in "The Strangest Secret":

> *The problem is that our mind comes as standard equipment at birth. It's free. And things that are given to us for nothing, we place little value on. Things that we pay money for, we value.*
>
> *The paradox is that exactly the reverse is true. Everything that's really worthwhile in life came to us free and our minds, our souls, our bodies, our hopes, our dreams, our ambitions, our intelligence, our love of family and children and friends and country. All these priceless possessions are free.*
>
> *But the things that cost us money are actually very cheap and can be replaced at any time.*

In other words, in order for us to grow, we need to grow ourselves. How do we grow? First, we are given the "limited telescopic view" of the world, as Solomon puts it. We have been placed in a world which embraces limitations in life, in everything that we do. Then, something within us urges us to find the "bigger picture": that is our instinct. All of us are born with important "free issue" of "equipment": our mind and free-will. What we do with our free issue is entirely up to us. We can either choose to believe that the limited view is all that there is, and that we do not have the ability nor the free will to change our limited view; or we can break free of the limitation that holds us back, the shackles that have kept us where we are up to this point. We can explore beyond our own chains.

Solomon said, "*Your life is as meaningful as your ability to reach out. It is this search that endows you.*" This corresponds well with Napoleon Hill's explanation of the word "educate". As Hill said in "Think and Grow Rich", "*That word is derived from the Latin word "educo," meaning to educe, to draw out, to DEVELOP FROM WITHIN.*" Solomon pointed out that in order for us to truly appreciate something, we need to go through our "experiential path" to reach "the other end." The search is in knowing and believing that we have the capability to achieve anything that we truly want to achieve, without violating the rights of others, to give us the satisfaction that we so desire. It is the basis of Hill's emphasis, "*Whatever the mind can conceive and believe, it can achieve.*" That is why Solomon said, "*Do not think of the target. Think of the process. Do not think of the bull's-eye. Think of the tension of the bow. Your heart will never lead you wrong. Leave the thought process behind. Don't send. Receive.*"

In "Magic in your Mind", the lesson on intuition is where Proctor, Morrissey and Gallagher taught us to listen to our instincts. This is when we let go of our reasoning, what we think as being logical, and just pay attention to what comes through. Moorjani said in "Dying to be Me":

> *I'm at my strongest when I'm able to let go, when I suspend my beliefs as well as disbeliefs, and leave myself open to all possibilities. That also seems to be when I'm able to experience the most internal clarity and synchronicities. My sense is that the very act of needing certainty is a hindrance to experiencing greater levels of awareness. In contrast, the process of letting go and releasing all attachment to any belief or outcome is cathartic and healing. The dichotomy is that for true healing to occur, I must let go of the need to be healed and just enjoy and trust in the ride that is life.*

This is reflected in Solomon's message to us: it's about the process.

> *Within every crisis, within every confrontation we have in our lives, within every obstacle we encounter, there is growth manifested at the same time. And I think that people need to be very creative in terms of being able to take that crisis, that obstacle – whatever you want to call it – and then turn that into Where is the growth from the experience? There is in that moment, in that crisis, growth to be mined. So it becomes much more creative than: I'm taking responsibility. What did I do to deserve this? What did you sign up for when you came into this lifetime? What were the challenges you set up for yourself? It isn't that you came to "experience" and just be. It's like you created a syllabus before you ever got here. Then, through your going through the syllabus, you have graduated into whatever level you want in terms of your growth. You laid out the obstacle course. You chose the circumstances in which you were born. You chose the things that you were going to have to confront. You made the hurdles higher.*

> *That's where the creation comes in. Before you ever were put into this plane. It's a challenge. Life is a challenge in the good sense. The challenge is for the participant to overcome these obstacles, and in the obstacles is growth. Transforming the energy that you have – the circumstances that you're having – and becoming more vivid in the living of it and more creative in the process of it. Joy comes through being able to handle a circumstance and create value out of it and move forward and let it propel you to higher levels. - Solomon*

Up until the age of 7, research has shown that our mind is similar to being in a perpetual hypnotic state. We absorbed anything and everything around us as the "truth", ranging from what our parents have told us through to what we sense around us.

We learned to explore since we were babies: we discovered our own hands, our feet, we learned how to crawl, stand and walk. Whenever we fell over when we learnt to walk, we didn't say, "That's it! I'm not meant to walk so why bother trying?!" We persisted, with our sheer will and determination, to get that toy that was out of reach, and we finally succeeded, despite our numerous failures. The ecstatic emotion that we felt when we finally achieved our goal - the one that we had been working so hard for – was also reflected in our parents' faces who continued to clap and encouraged us to walk further, pushing us beyond our limits. We knew no limits back then. We only knew of the destination. We didn't know how we would get there but we tried various ways to get that toy that we really wanted.

As adults, we have been conditioned to be satisfied and settle for less than what we have set ourselves up for. We convince ourselves that we are not meant to have it (whatever that goal or dream may be), thus failing to reach the destination that we wanted to get to. What is the difference between us now and who we were when we were just learning to walk? We believe in limitations now. We let fear and doubt control us. We let our own perceived limitations set the boundary for which we live in. Most of us have forgotten what it was like to push beyond our limits, and to feel the joy that came out of reaching our goals. The sense of achievement was what boosted our growth and self-esteem to move further on in life. Our ability to walk led us to be able to run and jump: we could do so much more on two feet rather than being on all four! Hill was correct when he said, *"Every adversity, every failure and every heartache carries with it the seed of an equivalent or greater benefit."*

If the purpose of the hurdles before us are to help us grow, the best way to start analysing our hurdles is as per Dyer's infamous quote:

Change the way you look at things, and the things you look at change.

There is always another way to look at the obstacle before you, remembering that it is only as temporary or as permanent as you make it to be. You can always choose to look at the obstacle from another angle, or from an aerial point of view; and you will see that there is always a way to overcome that hurdle. Your challenge is to use and exercise the mental faculties you were born with to overcome that obstruction before you. The satisfaction that you get from overcoming that obstruction is what gives you growth and helps you to move forward in life. You learn to trust and believe in yourself more as you conquer your obstacles. With each step towards success, you get a better glimpse of your connection to the infinite – to the immense power that lies within you.

Perhaps that is why we are born with the six gifts that Napoleon Hill discussed at great lengths about in "Think and Grow Rich": the gifts of imagination, intuition, will, memory, perception and reason. It is through the use of these gifts that we can dismantle the obstacles in our way, and we become more aligned with the greatness that we are.

As mentioned previously, I believe in reincarnation. I believe that we have set our syllabus of learning in this lifetime, with our soul contracts, and we help each other to realise our own potential on this plane. Since we are in a constant hypnotic state up until the age of about seven, I also believe that we chose the path that we were born into: our parents, our family and our environment. Our experiences as children help us to "learn our syllabus" in a more effective manner as we grow older. The most important thing is to recognise our lessons in this life, to recognise every hurdle and to be able to lift ourselves to see past the hurdle from another point of view, so that we can overcome it. The obstacle will never go away if we hide ourselves behind our fear and pretend that we do not see it: it is as good as an ostrich burying its head in the sand to hide from its predators. The hurdles are challenges we have set for ourselves to conquer. Until we analyse and solve the issue using our in-born gifts, the hurdles will continue to challenge us in this lifetime.

I am sure there will be people out there who say, "What about these children who are born with conditions? Or the ones who die as babies? What can they learn in such a short time frame?" I feel that the challenge there is not so much for the children, but more so for the adults and family members, particularly for those who have been left behind.

I recall a story, from about ten years ago, whereby a mother was walking with her almost twelve-month-old baby in a pram, when the pram was suddenly hit by a car and the baby flung out of the pram. I believe the baby was sent to the children's hospital but died soon after. This would have been a very sad story, if we choose to look at the misfortune that the parents had gone through. As it turned out, although the child died, his parents made the decision to donate his organs, and three other children who were in dire need for transplants finally got the organs that they needed to continue on with their lives. The parents of the child helped three other families lead happier lives through their own tragedy. One family learns that the soul of a child lives on, the other three families learn that there is love amongst us all, and that we are all interconnected. I recall seeing a video of the parents of the child who died, several months later, meeting the children and families of the children who received the transplants, and it struck me that tragedies are only as bad as we make it out to be for ourselves. There are lessons to be learned in everything that happens: question is, are we willing to learn it?

My personal story is that of my son's condition. I learnt, through him, that adversities are only as temporary or permanent as we allow them to be. He taught me that blame has its roots in fear, and as long as I succumb to that fear, I will never be able to experience my growth. Growth is realising that the obstacle before me is a step up for me to learn from.

When I first found out about his condition, I blamed it on the new trial vaccination that I had just prior to conceiving him. I blamed the last live virus vaccination that he had when his condition started to show up, within a week of the vaccination. My in-laws who normally didn't believe in mediums were told through one of their closest friends that it was part of his karma, and that there was a soul who was there to ensure that he will carry on with the suffering. They turned to writing out Buddhist scriptures because they were told that doing so will clear his soul of his past karma.

I have come to realise, after all my reading and research with what resonate with me, that we all come from a place of love. Beliefs that stem from fear, are beliefs that stem from the *lack of love*. There is no "someone" or "something" who ensures that we suffer in life, *unless* that is what we have signed up for in the first place to help us and those around us grow spiritually. Coming from a place of fear is something that has been driven into us by society. That is why we are afraid of going out of our comfort zone. Really, one should be asking his or herself, what contributes to my comfort zone? It is merely the result of our social conditioning from whence we were young, when we accepted everything as the truth about life.

You need to acknowledge these kinds of barricades and allow them to dissolve in front of you. Running into the barricade will not further your plan. You must allow them to find their space in existence and then dismiss that, without putting energy to it. You must ground yourself in a different kind of base, where the strength comes through the bottom of your life. It comes through you and out. You need to give yourself the time to develop this. If there has been conflict in your life, you need to create space around it. You need more space. You really are in control of that, but it has to start with your inner peace first. Inner peace is a rhythm of life. It is a connection with the universal energy, the cycle of it. Fears come from the fear of the responsibility of life. People don't want to have that responsibility. They want to be in a state of need. Somehow that (the need) becomes the generator for their existence, where in actuality, need is an obstruction. Need is what keeps us from connecting. There is a journey that happens, and eventually we become ourselves. This transition from a dependent to an independent, self-reliant individual.
– Solomon

Fear is something that most of us have to overcome in life in order to make progress in this lifetime. As Solomon mentioned, fear stems from our dismissal to take responsibility of our own lives. Our society has conditioned us to tell us that we always need someone or something else to fulfil our lives. On the contrary, that need is what stops us from taking full responsibility of all that is happening in our own life. Perhaps that is the paradox in life that we need to realise. We have come into this world, programmed the way that we wanted to be programmed so that we can elevate ourselves from the "issues" around us. We grow and increase our own vibration, to find the tune within us which harmonises with the universal symphony.

It is true what Price Pritchett said:

Usually it's in retrospect that you perceive their hidden logic and elegance.

I realised that blame and fear holds me back from moving forward in life. In fact, it keeps me rooted even deeper into fear. I finally accepted my son's condition as the universe's way of teaching me to cope and deal with fear, with its precision in the timing of events. Regardless of how it started, regardless of what we believe are the causes of his condition, he has brought the family closer together. I realised through my son that abundance is not limited to wealth. He revived my love for my family, for our health and well-being. He restored my faith in "miracles." He led me to discover Reconnective Healing and the invaluable lessons that came with it. I would probably say that if it were not for him, I would not have gone down this path of doing my own soul discovery and of self-growth. I would not have done all the research and readings that I have done to find out that we all co-exist together, in this intricate and beautiful tapestry of life, to help one another grow through life experience.

And so, I strongly urge you to look at your life currently. Think about all that you have gone through, all of your past and present experiences. Then take a step back, look from a higher point of view, from a loving perspective, and ask yourself, "What can I learn from my current situation?" You may not receive the answer immediately, but as long as you're continually being open minded and remain connected to your intuition, your connection to the universe, you will get your answer. Quoting Bob Proctor:

> *Prayer is when you're talking to God. Intuition is when God is talking to you.*

Are you willing to listen?

PART 4

My Analysis Thus Far

WE ARE INDIVIDUALS WORKING IN HARMONY TOGETHER

Everybody's individual existence is a symphony. – Solomon

Solomon's analogy of individuals as a symphony, playing in an even greater symphony truly resonates with me, due to my musical background. Those who know me well know that I always tend to be very expressive when I play. It is not because I force myself to do so: it is because I let myself go whenever I play. I really get into the feel of the music, allowing myself to move and flow to the sounds and rhythms that form the piece. I also enjoy composing music: the music that I compose is usually representative of my mood at that moment, something that I hear in my head, and then recreate physically through playing and writing. Being an electronic organ player, I would utilise all the instruments which harmonise well into my composition to create my pieces. Every instrument has different ranges and sounds: and I use that very difference to create my pieces via harmonisation of the groups of instruments. Even though each instrument is different, the mix of the individual instruments blend in very well to create a symphony. Music can also have varying tempos, but, through a conductor, everyone will be playing the same tune to the same tempo at the same time.

My basic understanding in music theory helps to guide me in the creation of my masterpiece: it tells me which cadences would work well, and which ones would not. It is up to my own free-will to create what I want; the rules will follow wherever I go. The piece that I'm creating may not work perfectly the very first time I write it out and play it back. Through exploration, I may decide to add something in or delete something else from my piece. In the end, it is through repetition, through trial and error, that I finally conceive my masterpiece. I feel joy during my creation process. I overflow with pride when I listen to my music at the end of the creation process, knowing all that I have overcome to get to the end of the piece. I feel triumphant and even greater joy when I see the other people's faces enjoying the music that I have created.

> *Your life is of That Which Is. It is a perfect thing, that which is in tune and in harmony with the music of the universe. It is a glorious symphony that every life conducts.* – Solomon

Everybody is here to create their own symphony. Yes, there are universal laws which govern us, just like the musical theory that governs how the music will turn out depending on what we do, but we are here as creators of our own lives. We are the composers of our own music, to create music which is in harmony with the universal symphony. First and foremost, however, we have to be aware that we *have the ability to be* the composer. The decision is ours. If we create our own music, we will vibrate to the tune that we create. If not, we will fit into the music that envelops us, the vibration that we are exposed to.

In order to be a creator, we must accept the responsibility in creating our own life, our own symphony. We need to understand that we are in charge, that we are in control of our own creation. We were in control from the very beginning, even before our conception.

Everything in the physical plane has been created twice: once in thought form, and then in physical form. First, we "hear" the music in our head. Then we do our best to recreate in physical form what we have "heard" in our head. We may not know the key of the piece. We may not know the entire storyline of the piece, but we make a start on our symphony by playing it and writing it down, and allowing ourselves to flow with the music. We make a start by *taking action*. We know the direction we're heading towards, and if we encounter detours along the way, we *know* they help us to create an even more melodious piece than the original one that we had in mind.

If we reach a "musical mental block" during the creation process, we need to stop, take a step (or two, or three) back, and assess how we have arrived at the hurdle. Perhaps we have used the wrong note, and the flow of the music did not work as well as we had anticipated. There is nothing wrong with going back and rearranging that harmonisation so that it fits into the overall piece which we have in mind. This is where Price Pritchett's "you^2" comes in:

Most of us can be found flying too close to the ground. Too often we don't give ourselves permission to soar. Seeking the quantum leap means violating the boundary of the probable. It means achieving well beyond the obvious. So don't limit your desires to what you think you "can have"... start going after what you "want." This means you must give yourself permission to dream, to risk. You must set yourself free. True, there are limits, but you don't need to worry about them. Your real limits are far beyond your artificial mental boundaries. The real limits won't box you in, but the false ones you're carrying around in your mind are a self-imposed prison. So how do you break out of that jail? Through surrender. You have to forfeit some of your old beliefs and sacrifice some of those "sensible" thinking patterns. So-called common sense can be a curse that puts a ceiling on how far you reach or how high you fly. you^2, the quantum leap strategy, is based on uncommon sense.

Pritchett mentions that we are too restrictive in what we do; too bounded by our own perceived limitations of ourselves. That is why we do not soar as high as we would have liked. Soaring is what we need to do if we are to go beyond our limited experiences. Soaring means pushing ourselves beyond the boundaries of our self-limitations, the jail that we have placed ourselves into. From a musical perspective, it means looking at it as an "overall picture" of what we are creating. Is it aligned with our original intention? Or has our music gone askew? Does the askew music still fit in? If so, we can always bring our music back to align with the original intention. We need to look at it from an external point of view (from where we are currently) because without an analysis of what we have done, we cannot determine where we are heading towards.

This does not mean that limitations are the bane of our lives. Limitations provide us with contrasts: sadness versus joy or love versus hatred. That is why we are here on earth with physical boundaries and limitations: it is to help facilitate the contrast in experiences that we feel. We're gifted with an ego, which in itself is a boundary because we can view anything from our own point of view and really go into the depths of our individual experience. Music has its limitations too: that is where the musical theory comes in. We can go from joy to sadness in our composition, by changing to the relative minor of the major key, for example. Music theory says that the relative minor follows the key signature of the major key, with the seventh note in the minor scale being a semitone higher than the major key. However, it is important to remember that limitations are there as our guides to help tell us what works and what doesn't. We are all gifted with imagination which allows us to escape from our perceived limitations, which are nothing more than our perception of the boundaries of our experiences.

When we have finally finished our first masterpiece, we look back at the effort it took and all that we have learnt during the process. We learned about what worked, what did not, and why. Most of all, we learnt that we are capable of being the creators of our life's experiences. As we expand our knowledge, we can go on to create even more masterpieces. We can help others to create their masterpiece by imparting some of our knowledge of what has worked (or has not worked) for us, so that they can hopefully achieve more in their lives.

It is unfortunate that most of us perceive ourselves as being the victim of our own lives. We view other people as being wealthier than us, smarter than us, more creative than us - all the reasons why everyone else is in a better position compared to us. Truth be told, these are not reasons at all: they are merely excuses we adopt because we are afraid of taking the responsibility for our own actions. We fear that we are not good enough. We fear that we may lose out. We fear being laughed at. We fear being mocked. We fear what others may think of us. In general, we live in a fearful world.

Fear leads to blame. We blame it on our upbringing. We blame it on the other person who caused us to go bankrupt. We blame it on our spouse who control us. We blame it on our lack of education. We blame it on our health. We blame it on the drugs which we took which gave us side effects. We blame the sun for giving us skin cancer.

What if we take a step back from this blaming habit that we are all guilty of, and look at our current issue from another point of view? Remember, Hoobyar et al showed us that our memory is not static: we can change our memory if we choose to do so.

Our obsessive-compulsive behaviour of blaming everyone and everything will only re-emphasise our past negative recollection, without any effort to improve the situation. Look at it this way, when you are angry at someone else, be it blaming them for something that they have done or not, you feel the anger within you. The situation may have already passed, but your recollection of the event invokes that anger within you each time you recall it. The other person doesn't feel it: the other person would not even care (unless you remind the person again, and again, and again). If you continually blame someone or something, you are continually pushing your responsibility to that particular person or situation. And each time you do so, the situation remains the same: it has already happened in the past, and quantum physics showed that although time can be reversed, the chances of it happening is extremely slim. The only person who is in charge of his or her own feelings is you. Only you can be responsible for letting go of the blame because only you are invoking the anger within yourself via your constant recollection. No one else is doing it for you.

Holding on to a past event which no longer serves us is representative of our unwillingness to let go of what has happened in the past – our unwillingness to take responsibility for what has happened in our lives and to move on from that point on. Using Doreen Virtue's words, we need to "*cut the cord*" with the past that is holding us back, after, we have learnt our lesson from it, whatever that may be. We have already paid for what has happened; we do not need to pay it twice.

Fear leads towards indecision. Indecision is another form of us passing on the responsibility of taking charge of our own lives onto someone or something else. We cannot decide what to do because we are afraid of making the wrong decision. We are indecisive about what we want to achieve in our lives, so we look to others to tell us what to do. Then, we remain static because everyone else around us is doing the same thing. We cannot grow if we remain static.

> *It doesn't matter which path you take. The important thing is to be on the path, because in that process you are ultimately trying to open doors. It's the process of opening doors that opens your life to the experience of that other plane. You're opening yourself to other possibilities... The important thing is that any spiritual path opens the door and makes you able to access whatever is to come. But you have to be in that process of opening doors. Trials make us stronger. – Solomon*

Most of us have been brought up to be humble, not to brag about ourselves. Regrettably, we take this learning one step too far, and think of ourselves as being unworthy, as being not enough. That is how we end up settling for less than what we wanted in the first place. We may want to make a difference in this world, but then we feel that it's only us and that no one else is interested, so we let go of our dream. We fear that no one else will support us in our cause, so we dismiss the idea, rendering it as useless. Solomon had this to say about self-worth:

> *Self-worth is not dictated by the amount of possession you obtain, or what you can hold on to. Self-worth is about an inner being being fulfilled, and allowing that joy to surface through its life. You're in the wrong program in a way in terms of how you believe your self-worth will surface. You have bought other people's predetermined menus for success. Don't be disheartened. You must learn to redefine for you what is true happiness. And that will come from the search, and journey into your heart. All the rest is avoidance. You're looking for someone to heal you. Healing comes from yourself, from inside you. The answers are already there. No one can make it better for you.*

True healing comes from within. Healing comes when we accept ourselves for who we are. Acceptance requires us to take responsibility for ourselves. It means we do not blame something or someone else for all that is happening within our lives. Healing occurs when we make decisions for ourselves. If we make a "mistake", we learn and correct them as we go along. Any door that we choose to walk through will take us down the same path - our path. We just need to walk through the door. We just need to move.

True healing requires us to listen to our instinct; we need to trust the intuition, the guidance that we are given. We need to experience it, not force it, and then let it go. To get to the core "issue", we need to start analysing our life from a point higher up the ladder, to get a bird's eye view of the hurdle. Whatever that is happening to us happens for a reason, and that reason is for us to grow. If we decide to ignore it, it will continually "be in our face" until we realise it and work out the solution to our hurdle. Our growth occurs when we use our creative abilities, our mental faculties that we are all born with, to solve the issues that we face, knowing that we are a part of the infinite universe.

Candace Pert spoke at length about our health: how it is affected by our food, environment, chemicals and the like. There may be truth to that and I do agree with her: we need to take care of our own body. However, I cannot help but feel that there is still a "blame factor" towards the end of her audiobook, "Your Body is Your Subconscious Mind." Listening to the interview, I still had the feeling that she was still giving her power away to an uncontrolled situation. She spoke about environmental and chemical toxins causing diseases in today's society, how we are all living in a world full of toxins, and I could not help but feel that there was still a shift in responsibility, as if it's not "my fault" that something "bad" has happened. I can somewhat understand her point of view. That was how I initially felt when I correlated the vaccinations (mine and my son's) to my son's condition. What I found, as I continued to blame my circumstances on situations beyond my control, was that I was sucked into a vortex of endless issues, which did nothing more than present even more problems to me. However, when I finally accepted the perfection of the universe, that everything happens for a reason, that nothing is accidental, I felt a shift in my vibration. Instead of a vortex of problems, I started to see the light at the end of the tunnel. Issues aren't the issue: it's our thinking of the issue which creates the issue. To solve it, we need to look beyond the issue, not continue to stare at the endless vortex issues.

I choose to look at the issue from another point of view: what if we chose the circumstance that we came in, and everything that happens around us is a by-product of our decision and free-will? In the perfection of the universe, everything occurs for a reason. In my case, I originally attributed my son's condition to the trial vaccine that I had just before conceiving him. That was me passing on the blame to someone else, giving my power away to a situation. Instead, I now choose to look at his condition from another perspective, from a loving perspective. I accept that my son would have the condition, at the right time, with the right "causes" from our physical world to trigger it in him. It may have been part of our soul contract that he comes into this world with a condition which would make me reassess my current situation at a particular point in time. In turn, my self-assessment would lead me to help others realise their purpose in life, including my own daughter who may be a "teacher" in the future. What if my son becomes a stronger person, not just physically but also spiritually, as a result of his condition? In this case, all three of us would experience our growth and increase our vibration, through one "unfortunate" situation.

I chose not to discuss at length about disease (or as many spiritual and motivational speakers call it, dis-ease) that we experience ourselves. I feel that there are other authors out there like Anita who can explain it better as they discuss at length about their own personal experiences and how they overcome their disease. On the other hand, I want us to assess the situation we are in. How has the other person's circumstance, illness or diagnosis affected the way we think and act? Is there a lesson for us in this, and if so, what is it? Is there something that we can do about this? If so, what can we do?

We are all interconnected in this tapestry of life; we all play a part in this majestic symphony of the infinite universe. We all exist in each other's lives because there is something that we can learn from one another, whether we realise this consciously or not. There are no "accidents"; there are only lessons to be learned and experienced. It all begins with our perspective in life: do we love ourselves sufficiently to view ourselves as an integral part of this symphony? Or do we feel insignificant, like the sixth viola in an orchestra, and that it does not matter whether we play our part or not. The truth is, although we may not feel like we're playing a vital role in the orchestra, an attentive listener can tune in to a missing part in the symphony, and sense that there is something that is lacking, making the symphony incomplete. So, no matter how trivial we think our lives may be, we still need to "play our part," that is, to be ourselves, forming a part of the infinite universe, and to learn, grow and experience our syllabus in this lifetime.

Moorjani explained it like this:

> *To me, this means seeing beauty in the journey and in the apparent mistakes as they take me to another level of understanding. My aim is to feel good enough about myself to get to a point of trust, and in that state, to let go of the outcome… letting go of attachment to any way of believing or thinking has made me feel more expanded and almost transparent so that universal energy can just flow through me. More positive coincidences happen in my life when I'm in this state of allowing. We always attract the perfect results, and like calls to like.*

I challenge all of us to re-look at our situation from another point of view, from a loving perspective, and assess our learnings to be had from that seemingly unfortunate situation. The situation may be trivial, but we ask ourselves, "Is there something that I can learn from this? How can I improve on this situation?" We are here to be ourselves, and to empower ourselves to grow and experience the vibrations that exist on this plane.

Empowerment does not mean telling others that they are wrong and that we are correct. It does not mean showing off to others that we are better because we are smarter, or that we are multi-talented or that "our faith is better than their faith." Empowerment in that sense stems from fear, and in essence, is more about controlling others. A fear based empowerment relates to our ego, our need to convince everyone else that that we are correct, because the very act of trying to convince others is dictating others to accept your thoughts and opinions. Empowerment that stems from love is one where we accept ourselves for who we truly are and then moving forth from that point onwards. We accept that everyone else is different, yet we are all the same as we are all part of the one universe, the one infinite. True empowerment that stems from love is one where we do not have to prove who we are: the truth is already within us, and we radiate that truth outwards, so much so that those around us feel the love that comes from within us. By radiating love outwards to those around us, we become the instruments of love that we are, because, in essence, we are an extension of the universe that is made of love.

The truth, as I understand it, is that we are all different expressions of the one infinite universe, the "one mind" in this realm. We inspire one another through our own self-expression and we remind ourselves of our own individual power when we become inspired by those whom we come into contact with, whether they are celebrities or just "plain" people whom we know in our lives. Inspiration is a way of reminding us what we have forgotten about our true selves in this realm. If we pay attention to our own lives, we can see inspiration all around us. It is all a matter of perception and "waking up" our current reality to change our own vibration, our own frequency, to realise this within us.

I first began realising this fact when I look at my own children, my husband, my parents, and those around me. The one theme I noticed most often is that children, especially when they are young, remind parents of their true selves from when they were younger. It may be that they serve to remind us of our own capabilities which we have suppressed through being in this physical realm. How we react to the behaviour is a matter of our perception, our embracement of their "different" behaviour. Should we choose to fight and suppress their "defiant" behaviour, they may just grow up to be like us in the future and we may see the same theme occur over and over through the generations in our lifetime. If we embrace it, we may just learn something about them, and about ourselves, that we never realised was ever within us. It is all a matter of perception, embracing that which is a part of ourselves, experiencing the web of existence for ourselves (which we forgot about through the years of being on the physical plane) and then moving on from that point onwards.

When we are at one with who we truly are, and we become the instruments of who we are, we vibrate at the frequency which allows the universe to support us. The support in the universal frequency can be assimilated to a transition in the quantum field where we "suddenly" attract what we need in order to continue with our pursuit in life. Some people know this as the "Law of Attraction." A recent example of this is what I saw of my Facebook feed on one computer screen, whilst I was typing away on this manuscript about becoming the instruments of love that we are, on another screen. A friend posted a YouTube tribute to Michael Jackson whereby a duo from India got together child prodigies from around the world to contribute to the video, playing and singing, "Heal the World." I never really paid attention to the lyrics of the song until just then, and I was very touched by the universal support that I am getting by writing this manuscript, as the lyrics fit in with what I was trying to express in words. You can check out the video here for yourself:
https://www.youtube.com/watch?v=h6d6Yo3DwVI

Taking an excerpt from "**Heal the World**" lyrics by Michael Jackson:

There's a place in your heart
And I know that it is love
And this place could be much
Brighter than tomorrow
And if you really try
You'll find there's no need to cry
In this place you'll feel
There's no hurt or sorrow

There are ways to get there
If you care enough for the living
Make a little space
Make a better place

Heal the world
Make it a better place
For you and for me
And the entire human race
There are people dying
If you care enough for the living
Make it a better place
For you and for me

If you want to know why
There's love that cannot lie
Love is strong
It only cares of joyful giving
If we try we shall see
In this bliss we cannot feel
Fear of dread
We stop existing and start living

We could fly so high
Let our spirits never die
In my heart I feel you are all my brothers
Create a world with no fear
Together we cry happy tears
See the nations turn their swords into plowshares

Here are some other songs that have inspired me, particularly as I was writing my manuscript.

"Greatest Love of All"
by Michal Masser (music) and Linda Creed (lyrics):

Everybody's searching for a hero
People need someone to look up to
I never found anyone who fulfils my needs
A lonely place to be
So I learned to depend on me

I decided long ago, never to walk in anyone's shadows
If I fail, if I succeed
At least I'll live as I believe
No matter what they take from me
They can't take away my dignity
Because the greatest love of all
Is happening to me
I found the greatest love of all
Inside of me
The greatest love of all
Is easy to achieve
Learning to love yourself
It is the greatest love of all

> *And if by chance, that special place*
> *That you've been dreaming of*
> *Leads you to a lonely place*
> *Find your strength in love*

I first understood the meaning of "Greatest Love of All" when we sang it at the study course that I attended when I was still in primary school. It meant a lot to me as Dr. Ng was trying to instil into us the need to be able to love ourselves and "make it on our own." Although it was simplistic back then, it has taken on a deeper meaning for me now. Through my research and this manuscript, through sorting out my thoughts on what I have learnt almost thirty years on, I have come to realise that we are made of love, and that we all have this ability to look within for answers to the questions that we have. And as the lyrics go, if that special place does not lead us to where we thought we were heading, we need to find our own strength, to persist on until our dream is achieved.

As Solomon pointed out many times throughout the book, it is in the process that we go through to achieve what we want where we learn the most about ourselves, our capability, our strengths; it is the process which gives us the true satisfaction that our spiritual being so desires as we look back upon all that we have conquered to make our dream a reality. This is where another song really resonates with me each time I sing-a-long with it.

"One Moment in Time"
written by Albert Hammond and John Bettis:

> *Each day I live*
> *I want to be*
> *A day to give*
> *The best of me*
> *I'm only one*
> *But not alone*
> *My finest day*
> *Is yet unknown*
>
> *I broke my heart*
> *Fought every gain*
> *To taste the sweet*
> *I face the pain*
> *I rise and fall*

> *Yet through it all*
> *This much remains*
>
> *I want one moment in time*
> *When I'm more than I thought I could be*
> *When all of my dreams are a heartbeat away*
> *And the answers are all up to me*
> *Give me one moment in time*
> *When I'm racing with destiny*
> *Then in that one moment of time*
> *I will feel*
> *I will feel eternity*

As the song goes, I feel eternity with me as I go ahead to reach for what I want, to live the way that I want. The universe, with its infinite potential is always with me: I only need to tap into this wealth of knowledge that is omnipotent, listen to my intuition as that is the universal guidance for me, and I will find myself fully supported wherever I may be. I know this for a fact: throughout the time, as I wrote my manuscript, I felt guided towards relevant resources at each step of the way, as I penned every chapter which made up the manuscript. Knowing this gives me the confidence to believe that everything will be revealed, as we progress, at the right time, at the right place.

In order for everything to "fall into place", I needed to have faith that it will happen and to have the determination to carry on with my goal. This is where Abraham's "workshop of the mind" comes in: this is where we focus in detail exactly what we want. If we truly believe that what we want already exists in a vibrational reality somewhere in the future (remembering that time is not linear in the infinite world), that vibration is the universe calling out to us in the vibrational form of an idea. When we act on the idea, we follow our instinct: this is where we vibrate at the same vibration as the idea, or as Proctor normally refers to as the "Y-Y vibration". When that happens, it is vitally important that we do not "kill off our own idea" by convincing ourselves that it will not work, because the act of doing so puts us in a conflicting vibration or where the "X" or old vibration takes over. This is the first step which stops our goals from becoming a reality because it is when we doubt our instinct. In this instance, Abraham advises that we "meditate", that is, we allow the universe to guide us and show us the way whilst having faith that our goal *will* happen.

Through my personal experience, I find that I need to strike a balance between being consciously aware of the details of my goals, and surrendering to the universe. Such balance is necessary to propel me forward quicker than it would have taken me if I were to do everything consciously, step by step, through my own limited knowledge. This is because Abraham describes the hunch or idea as *"…the source calling you on the path of least resistance to the full realisation of it."* As such, I need to fully trust that I will get there, which means that I need to have the will and determination to persevere whenever it seems as if what I want is not happening in my life. As Napoleon Hill said:

> *Faith is the head chemist of the mind. When faith is blended with the vibration of thought, the subconscious mind instantly picks up the vibration, translates it into its spiritual equivalent, and transmits it to the infinite intelligence, as in the case of prayer.*

You have to understand that you cannot have faith and fear at the same time; you can only have one or the other.

Abraham reinforced Hill's idea:

> *Every subject is really two subjects: wanted and the absence of what is wanted. And you are in the vicinity of one or the other usually.*

In other words, only one emotion, one vibration can dominate at each time: wanted or absence of wanted. Faith with love or fear with absence of love. Harmonisation or dis-harmonisation with the universal vibration. That is why faith is of utmost importance in realising our goals, our manifestations. Faith is the vibration that keeps us in synchronisation with universal intelligence and our goals. Faith shows us the way. Faith clears the fog in our path to help us reach our destination through the path of least resistance. Faith is that which helps us to harmonise with universal symphony.

I have learnt through my personal experience with Reconnective Healing that we are all interconnected to one another. I have personally experienced what Dr. Dyer meant by breaking the bonds when one is connected to spirit. Unlike Reiki and Qi Gong practitioners who send energy to another being in order to heal a person, RH practitioners are taught to receive, not send. Hence, unlike other energetic modality practitioners who normally feel tired at the end of a session, I concur with Dr Pearl: I actually feel more energetic after conducting a session. At first I thought that the only difference was because I was receiving the energy, light and information, not sending it. However, after conducting several sessions and through my readings and research, I find that it may be more than that. It may also be because the client and myself are connected to the one mind, the infinite universe whenever I facilitate RH. It is as if the energy, light and information exchange occurs on that plane, not in the physical plane that we live in. Through my debriefing with my clients, I find that they experience more when I am more connected to them, when the conduit that I am is clear and at one with the client, when I am more aware of the client being with me in oneness. In turn, their experiences are normally beyond what words can describe on this plane.

It seems that when we are more connected to spirit, as Dyer puts it, the more aware we are of all that goes on. That is because when we are connected to the universe, we are connected to all and everything. When that happens, we are in vibration with the universe, and that means that whatever we need to carry out our work here on earth will also be on the same vibration and be provided to us when we need it. Faith ensures that we remain in that vibration to obtain what we need. Hence, the only thing that stops us from getting what we require is being out of sync with the universal vibration, being at disharmony with the infinite universe.

YOU ARE THE SUN

Rediscover you. – Joanne Ong

Disassembling the word *universe* into *uni-verse*: we are many, yet we all work as one, together in perfect harmonisation, in the symphonic world that we live in. We all play a part in the symphony. We all play a similar, yet, slightly different tune to one another. Whilst we play, we may only be aware of our own part of the symphony, but when we become aware of the orchestra that is also playing together with us, we become aware of the crucial component that our part plays in harmonising with the orchestra. That is when we realise the potential that we have within us to make a difference to those whose lives we "touch".

An example of how a young cancer patient helped the rest of the patients in the cancer ward in which she spent most of her time in is a prime example of realising our own capabilities and helping others to elevate their vibration at the same time. Perhaps this is what Eric Pearl meant by calling his book "The Reconnection: Heal Yourself, Heal Others." In Wayne Dyer's book entitled, "Inspiration: Your Ultimate Calling," he gave an example of a young girl with cancer by the name of Cassie, who wrote to "Extreme Makeover: Home Edition" asking the team to help makeover the dreary cancer ward which she spent a lot of her time in. The end result was that the ward was turned into a fairyland and playground, but more importantly, something miraculous happened to the children who helped with the renovation:

> Without exception, all of the children in the cancer ward who participated in the renovation had their white cells increase in the direction of well-being and away from the damaging cancer in their bodies. Imagine – by moving more into harmony with Spirit and using this newfound

> *inspiration to take action in the service of other children, the actual process of returning to perfect health was activated. The healing power within these young people somehow miraculously responded to the results and actions of Cassie's inspiration by increasing their white cells!*

This further emphasises my theory, my belief: that nothing happens by accident. Everything occurs in perfect timing, and for a reason. Whether we fight the situation that we are in with lower vibrations or we embrace whatever it is that comes our way, accept it, experience it, and then move on with the knowledge that we have the power to influence our lives and the lives of others-it is entirely up to us. We have the power. We have free will. We can make our own life choices.

On your own, you may not be aware of the power that you have in other people's lives. You may not realise how crucial you are in the scheme of things. Perhaps we have all come here to recognise our individuality in this world whilst helping one another to elevate our vibrational levels, to elevate the universal vibration to another level. In doing so, we would be able to recognise our own abilities and feel the power of the universe on an individual level, as shown by Cassie.

You have been forced to forget who you were when you were born, so that you may realise the power within you, on your own accord. After all, our purpose lies not in reaching our goals since we are a part of the infinite, but in remembering our connection to the universe, and in our self-discovery of the power that we all have within us. It is in the process that we discover our inner abilities, and realise our connection to the infinite once again, so that we may carry out our purpose here on this plane. Hence, what is important is not that we reach our destination, so much so that our journey to our destination helps us to recognise our own power and helps us with our individual growth which in turn, helps to elevate the universal vibration that we are all a part of.

You are a part of the infinite universe. You are an expression of the infinite mind, the uni-verse. You can always tap into the infinite power within: you only need to be aware of your capabilities.

Understand that you are the sun which shines onto all around you. You are the centre of the universe, and the universe revolves around you, just as it revolves around others as well. We may not be able to perceive the intricacies of the universe with our limited understanding on this plane, so this is where faith comes into play. Faith is when we know that we are connected to the infinite and that everything is made available to us at precise timing. Trust is knowing that it will happen. We need to trust in the laws of the universe to provide for us, just as we trust that the law of gravity to holds us down on this plane.

You are a creator of your own life: good or bad. Know that you are infinite and that you have access to the infinite source of energy to create whatever you want in life. You are interconnected to all that you require to grow, on this plane, and beyond. You are not alone: you do not only affect your own life. Like the sun, your presence is felt by everyone else. You can be whatever you set yourself out to be. So go forth and set yourself to bring out the best in others around you. You are here to be YOU. The universe will align itself to suit your needs, such that you become the centre of your own universe, and yet, you are tied to the infinite universe at the same time.

Awaken yourself to the infinity that you are.

Awaken your inner potential to discover THE SUN WITHIN.

It is time to REDISCOVER YOU.

REFERENCES

Pearl, E and Ponzlov, F, 2013. *Solomon Speaks on Reconnecting Your Life.* Hay House, Inc. E-book.

Pearl, E, 2013. *The Reconnection: Heal Others, Heal Yourself.* Hay House. E-book.

Pearl, E, 2016. *Reconnective Healing Level I and II seminar*, Sydney.

Proctor, B. Various online sources and seminars.

Moorjani, A, 2012. *Dying to Be Me: My Journey from Cancer, to Near Death, to True Healing.* Hay House. E-book.

Moorjani, A, 2016. *What If This Is Heaven?: How Our Cultural Myths Prevent Us from Experiencing Heaven on Earth.* Hay House Inc. E-book.

Ng, L. 1990. *"A" Star Student Seminar.*

Hill, N. *Think and Grow Rich.* Various online sources.

Nightingale, E. T*he Strangest Secret.*

Dyer, W. 2010. *Inspiration: Your Ultimate Calling.* Hay House. E-book.

Rudd, R. 2013. *The Gene Keys: Unlocking the Higher Purpose Hidden in your DNA.* Watkins Publishing. E-book.

The Bible. Online sources.

Tagore, R. Poem.

Hurtak, J.J. 1977. The Academy for Future Science. *The Book of Knowledge: The Keys of Enoch®.* www.keysofenoch.org

Moore, D. 2015. *The Developing Genome: An Introduction to Behavioral Epigenetics*. Oxford University Press. E-book.

Schwartz, G. 2008. *The Energy Healing Experiments: Science Reveals Our Natural Power to Heal*. Atria Books.

Strong's Greek Dictionary. Google.

Dossey, L. 2014. *One Mind: How Our Individual Mind Is Part of a Greater Consciousness and Why It Matters*. Hay House, Inc.

Pritchett, P. 2012. you2: *A High Velocity Formula for Multiplying Your Personal Effectiveness in Quantum Leaps*. Pritchett & Associates.

McTaggart, L. 2008. *The Intention Experiment: Use Your Thoughts to Change the World*. Harper Element. E-book.

Kuhn, G. 2013. *How Quantum Physicists Build New Beliefs*. E-book.

June 23rd, 2016. Dr. Wayne Dyer's Life After Death. Elevated Existence. [online] Available at: http://www.elevatedexistence.com/dr-wayne-dyers-life-after-death/

Epilogue Lyrics from Les Miserables.

Hicks, A. Various online sources.

Pert, C. 2004. *Your Body Is Your Subconscious Mind*. Sounds True; Unabridged edition. Audiobook.

Dotz, T, Hoobyar, T, Sanders, S. 2013. *NLP: The Essential Guide to Neuro-Linguistic Programming*. William Morrow Paperbacks.

Lipton, B. 2016. *The Biology of Belief 10th Anniversary Edition: Unleashing the Power of Consciousness, Matter & Miracles*. Hay House, Inc.

Wattles, W. Various online sources.

Allen, J. Various online sources.

Behrand, G. *Your Invisible Power*. E-book.

Radin, D. 2009. *The Conscious Universe: The Scientific Truth of Psychic Phenomena*. HarperOne.

Emoto, M. 2011. *The Hidden Messages in Water*. Atria Books. E-book.

Emoto, M. 2006. *Water Crystal Healing: Music and Images to Restore Your Well-Being*. Atria Books.

Loewenstein, W. 2013. *Physics in Mind: A Quantum View of the Brain*. Basic Books.

Grout, P. 2013. *E-Squared: Nine Do-It-Yourself Energy Experiments That Prove Your Thoughts Create Your Reality*. Hay House Insights. E-book.

Group, P. 2014. *E-Cubed: Nine More Energy Experiments That Prove Manifesting Magic and Miracles Is Your Full-Time Gig*. Hay House. E-book.

Ziglar, Z. Various sources online.

Jackson, M. Lyrics from *Heal the World*. [online] Available at: https://www.youtube.com/watch?v=h6d6Yo3DwVI

Masser, M and Creed, L. Lyrics from *The Greatest Love of All*. Sung by Houston, W.

Bettis, J. Lyrics from *One Moment in Time*. Sung by Houston, W.

ACKNOWLEDGEMENTS

I would like to take this opportunity to acknowledge all the soul contracts who have been a part of my life, whether in this physical world or in the spiritual realm. My journey has been an interesting one and I thank everyone for making it what it is, to give me the experience that I needed to have in order to write and publish this book.

Thank you to the universe, my guides and angels, for your support the whole time, and for not giving up on me. Thank you, Sebel, for everything.

Thank you to all the authors for their permission to mention and quote them in my book. I am truly grateful for coming across their materials; they have really guided me along the way.

Thank you, Judy for the lovely foreword to my book. You truly are an inspirational being.

Thank you to my children for being patient with this "hot-headed" mummy who always wants things done her way. Thank you too for showing me what life really means.

Last but not least, thank you to my husband who is always there for me whenever I feel like giving up or when things don't seem to work out my way. Thank you for giving me the space to allow for my introspection and thank you for not making fun of my ideas and comments all throughout the years. Thank you for your support and your belief in me.

THANK YOU TO ALL
Who have been a part of my life
A part of my journey
A part of my strife
A part of my glory
A part of my drive.

WITHOUT YOU
There would be no hope
There would be no me;
I would not cope
I'd fail to be me.

MAY WE ALL
Continue to grow
Continue to expand
Continue to draw
On the lessons we have learned.

ABOUT THE AUTHOR

Joanne Ong was born in Malaysia but spent most of her life in Australia, where she now resides with her husband and two children. She has a double degree in Engineering and Commerce, and diplomas in music. She enjoys writing poems, playing and composing music, and reading, but most of all, she loves to learn and help others to achieve their goals. Joanne is an engineer, a Reconnection Certified Practitioner, a consultant with the Proctor Gallagher Institute, a wife and a mother. Her mission is to awaken and empower individuals to heal their lives, so that they can live their lives with an abundance of love, joy and gratitude, knowing that they are the creators of their own destiny.

Please visit
www.joanne-ong.com
and
www.rediscover-you.net

www.ingramcontent.com/pod-product-compliance
Lightning Source LLC
Chambersburg PA
CBHW051806040426
42446CB00007B/548